# CONTENTS

| | | | |
|---|---|---|---|
| **DVD Menu Screens** | | | **08** |
| **Introduction** | | | **10** |
| **My Language – Influences and Attitudes** | | | **11** |

| | | Page | DVD Links |
|---|---|---|---|
| Teachers' Notes | | 12 | |
| My Language | Starting to Think About Language – Voicing Your Opinion | 13 | ✔ |
| | Teenagers Talking – Views & Attitudes | 15 | ✔ |
| | What is Accent? What is Dialect? | 16 | ✔ |
| | The Difference Between Standard English and Received Pronunciation | 17 | ✔ |
| | Translating the News | 18 | ✔ |
| | Standard English – the Great Debate | 19 | |
| | Language and Belonging | 21 | ✔ |
| | Your Unique Language – Where Does it Come From? | 24 | |
| | A Pie Chart of Your Personal Language (Idiolect) | 25 | |
| Extension Activities | A Day in My Language Life | 26 | |
| | My Language | 27 | |

**Telling a Story – From Talk to Text**     **29**

| | | Page | DVD Links |
|---|---|---|---|
| Teachers' Notes | | 30 | |
| Telling a Story | Stories You Tell | 31 | |
| | Spoken Stories | 32 | |
| Option 1 – Sevim's Story | Sevim's Spoken Story | 33 | ✔ |
| | Sevim's Story in Writing | 35 | |
| Option 2 – Tim's Story | Tim's Spoken Story | 38 | ✔ |
| | Tim's Story in Writing | 40 | |
| A Written Story | Writing Your Own Story | 43 | |
| | Summing Up What You Have Learned | 43 | |

© English and Media Centre, 2008

# Contents

## Keeping in Touch – Texts, Emails, Blogs & Letters — 45

|  |  | Page | DVD Links |
|---|---|---|---|
| Teachers' Notes |  | 46 |  |
| Keeping in Touch | A First Look at the Texts | 47 |  |
|  | Comparing Two Texts | 47 |  |
|  | Communication at the Beginning of the 21st Century | 48 |  |
|  | A Continuum Line | 49 |  |
| Simulation | A Guide to Keeping in Touch | 49 |  |
| Charts |  | 50 |  |
| Texts |  | 52 |  |

## Texts For Tots – The Language of Picture Books — 55

*(19 mins)*

|  |  | Page | DVD Links |
|---|---|---|---|
| Teachers' Notes |  | 56 |  |
| Where the Wild Things Are | Reading the Words | 57 |  |
|  | Reading the Whole Story | 58 |  |
|  | Looking More Closely | 59 |  |
|  | Tracking Words and Images – Chart | 61 |  |
| John Brown, Rose and the Midnight Cat | A Close Look at Sentences | 62 |  |
|  | Sentence Types | 63 |  |
|  | Writing the End of the Story | 64 |  |
|  | Summing Up What You Have Learned | 64 |  |
|  | Reading Other Picture Books | 64 |  |
| Learning to Read | Babies With Books | 65 | ✔ |
|  | Your Own Memories | 66 |  |
|  | Your Ideas About Reading | 66 |  |
|  | Reading Strategies | 67 | ✔ |
| Creative Writing | Writing a Picture Book of Your Own | 68 |  |
| Extension Activities | The Language of Peter Rabbit | 70 |  |
|  | Writing Your Own Adaptation | 71 |  |

## Mathilda Speaking – Learning to Talk — 73

|  |  | Page | DVD Links |
|---|---|---|---|
| Teachers' Notes |  | 74 |  |
|  | Language Points to Draw Out in Each Clip | 75 |  |
|  | Language Development Milestones | 77 |  |
| Mathilda Speaking | Learning to Talk | 79 |  |
| Watching Mathilda | A First Viewing | 80 | ✔ |
|  | Tracking Mathilda's Language Development – Chart | 82 |  |

4    LANGUAGE WORKS    © English and Media Centre, 2008

# Contents

| | | | |
|---|---|---|---|
| Developing Children's Language | Charting Mathilda's Progress – Chart | 83 | |
| | What Bonny Does | 84 | |
| | Helping Your Child to Speak – a Guide for Parents | 85 | |

## Playing With Words – Games to Explore Language — 87

| | | Page | DVD Links |
|---|---|---|---|
| Teachers' Notes | | 88 | |
| One Hundred Words – 3 Variations | 1. A Sorting Game | 89 | |
| | 2. Lucky Dip | 91 | |
| | 3. Words and Sentences | 92 | |
| | The Words | 93 | |
| Squabble | Basic and Advanced Versions | 95 | |
| Word Class Rush | Versions 1 and 2 | 96 | |
| Lingo | Version 1 | 97 | |
| | An Alternative Lingo | 97 | |
| | Cards | 98 | |
| Puns, Playing With Words and Misunderstandings | Student Sheet | 99 | |
| | Cards | 100 | |
| | Joke Cards | 101 | |

## The Apprentice – How Groups Talk — 103

| | | Page | DVD Links |
|---|---|---|---|
| Teachers' Notes | | 104 | |
| Alan Sugar's Apprentices | Before Watching | 105 | |
| | Deciding the Group Name | 106 | ✔ |
| | Discussing the Groups – Statements | 107 | |
| Planning the Great Ormond Street Calendar | Looking More Closely – Analysing the Discussion | 108 | ✔ |
| | Framework 1 – The Roles People Take | 109 | |
| | Framework 2 – Conversation Analysis | 111 | |
| | Framework 3 – Non-Verbal Communication | 113 | |
| | Sharing Groups | 115 | |
| Re-wind | Re-writing the Script | 115 | |
| | Transcripts | 116 | |
| Year 9 Apprentices | | 121 | |
| | Planning the Calendar | 122 | ✔ |
| | Pitching the Idea | 123 | ✔ |
| Simulation – Cash and Choice | Stage A – Discussion and Decision Making | 124 | |
| | Stage B – The Presentations | 125 | |
| | Stage 3 – Reflecting on Group Work | 125 | |

© English and Media Centre, 2008

## Cocoa Bean – Words That Sell · 127

|  |  | Page | DVD Links |
|---|---|---|---|
| Teachers' Notes |  | 128 |  |
| Words That Sell | Painting a Picture, Selling Products | 129 |  |
|  | Arresting Language | 130 |  |
| Cocoa Bean Case Study | How We Got Started | 131 | ✔ |
|  | The Early Days | 131 | ✔ |
|  | Examples of Labels and Packaging (2002) | 132 |  |
|  | Cocoa Bean Packaging | 133 | ✔ |
|  | Admiring Innocent | 133 | ✔ |
|  | Innocent Smoothie Packaging | 134 |  |
|  | New Packaging | 135 |  |
|  | Working on the Words | 135 | ✔ |
|  | Wild and Classic | 135 | ✔ |
|  | Looking More Closely | 135 | ✔ |
|  | Wild and Classic Packaging | 136 |  |
|  | Inside the Packaging | 137 | ✔ |
|  | All Change! | 138 |  |
| Simulation | Marketing Cocoa Bean Lollipops | 140 |  |
|  | Lollipop Label – Role-Play | 141 |  |

## What's Cool? Digging For Words · 145

|  |  | Page | DVD Links |
|---|---|---|---|
| Teachers' Notes |  | 146 |  |
| How Language Changes | Investigating the Ways Words Change | 147 |  |
|  | Over to You | 150 |  |
|  | McJob – Challenging the OED | 150 |  |
| Becoming a Word Archaeologist | Before Watching | 151 |  |
|  | Watching 'Cool' | 151 | ✔ |
|  | After Watching | 151 |  |
|  | Investigating a Word | 152 |  |

## Contents

### Cooking the Books – Language Through Time — 155

| | | Page | DVD Links |
|---|---|---|---|
| Teachers' Notes | | 156 | |
| Language Through Time | A First Activity | 157 | |
| | What Recipe Books Used to be Like – a Typical Recipe | 158 | |
| | Annotated Text | 159 | |
| | Comparing Texts – Bread and Butter Pudding | 160 | |
| | Why Have Recipe Books Changed? | 160 | |
| | Trying out the Recipes | 160 | |
| | Why Have Recipe Books Changed? Chart | 161 | |
| | The Recipe Texts | 162 | |
| Cooks on TV | | 168 | |
| | What's Changed? | 169 | ✔ |
| | Cooks on TV – Chart | 170 | |
| | Suggestions for Your Own Writing | 171 | |
| Extension Activities | What's a Pudding? | 172 | |
| | A Parody of Food Programmes – Posh Nosh | 173 | |

# DVD Menu Screens

## 1. My Language – Influences and Attitudes

| Selectable button | Duration | Onscreen section title | See page |
|---|---|---|---|
| Voicing your opinion | 1 min 30 | | 13 |
| Teenagers talking | 5 mins | Family | 15 |
| | | Making judgements | |
| | | Adapting your speech | |
| What is accent/dialect? | 3 mins 45 | An expert view | 16 |
| | | Teenagers on dialect | |
| Talking posh *(The difference between Standard English and RP)* | 3 mins | An expert view | 17 |
| | | Channel 4 News | |
| | | ITV News | |
| Translating the news | 45 secs | | 18 |
| Language and belonging | 3 mins 15 | Tony Blair | 23 |
| | | Shifting your language | |
| | | Getting it wrong – *The Catherine Tate Show* | |

## 2. Telling a Story – From Talk to Text

| Selectable button | Duration | Onscreen section title | See page |
|---|---|---|---|
| Sevim's story | 50 secs | | 33 |
| Tim's story | 50 secs | | 38 |

## 3. Keeping in Touch – Texts, Emails, Blogs & Letters    No DVD

## 4. Texts for Tots – the Language of Picture Books

| Selectable button | Duration | Onscreen section title | See page |
|---|---|---|---|
| Babies with books | 2 mins 30 | | 65 |
| Learning to read *(Reading strategies)* | 5 mins | | 67 |

## 5. Mathilda Speaking – Learning to Talk

| Selectable button | Duration | Onscreen section title | See page |
|---|---|---|---|
| In the high chair – 12 months | 45 secs | | 80 |
| Reading with Mum – 15 months | 1 min | | |
| Scarf and beads – 20 months | 1 min 10 | | |
| Sticklebrick car – 24 months | 1 min 10 | | |
| Let's pretend – 24 months | 1 min 10 | | |
| Turning off the light – 25 months | 40 secs | | |
| Talking to herself – 28 months | 40 secs | | |
| Talking with friends – 2 years, 7 months | 2 mins 30 secs | | |

LANGUAGE WORKS © English and Media Centre, 2008

# DVD Menu Screens

### 6. Language Games    No DVD

### 7. The Apprentice – How Groups Talk

|  | Selectable button | Duration | Onscreen section title | See page |
|---|---|---|---|---|
| Alan Sugar's apprentices | Deciding the group name | 4 mins |  | 106 |
|  | Planning the calendar | 5 mins |  | 108 |
| Year 9 apprentices | Planning the calendar | 4 mins | Deciding on a name | 122 |
|  |  |  | Deciding on a slogan |  |
|  |  |  | Planning the calendar |  |
|  | Pitching the idea | 5 mins | Planning the pitch | 123 |
|  |  |  | Making the pitch |  |
|  |  |  | Re-making the pitch |  |
|  | Reflections on leadership | 1 min 30 |  | N/A |

### 8. Cocoa Bean – Words that Sell

| Selectable button | Duration | Onscreen section title | See page |
|---|---|---|---|
| How we got started | 40 secs |  | 131 |
| Our packaging | 1 min |  | 133 |
| Admiring Innocent | 1 min |  | 133 |
| Working on the words | 2 mins 30 | Choosing the right words | 135 |
|  |  | Standing out from the crowd |  |
|  |  | A close look at language |  |
| Wild and Classic | 3 mins | Wild chocolate | 135 |
|  |  | Classic chocolate |  |
|  |  | Naughty but nice |  |
| Inside the packaging | 45 secs |  | 137 |

### 9. What's Cool? Digging for Words

| Selectable button | Duration | Onscreen section title | See page |
|---|---|---|---|
| Where 'cool' comes from | 11 mins 30 |  | 151 |

### 10. Cooking the Books – Language through Time

| Selectable button | Duration | Onscreen section title | See page |
|---|---|---|---|
| Fanny Craddock – 1966 | 4 mins |  | 168 |
| Jamie Oliver – 1999 | 4 mins |  | 168 |
| Nigella Lawson – 2002 | 4 mins |  | 168 |

© English and Media Centre, 2008

# Introduction

## Learning to use language, learning about language

This publication is all about language – how it is used in the world, how it has changed over time, how we acquire it, how we play with it, how we use it creatively and inventively to make things happen. It brings together both the excitement of finding out about language and reflection about what this might tell students about their own language use. As such, it encourages them not only to become better users of language but also to develop their thinking and knowledge, which is an integral part of that process. The publication is about more than a narrow idea of the 'functional', offering a fuller and richer perspective on what this means. 'Fully functional' approaches allow students to think for themselves, apply knowledge and make it their own, as well as motivating them to work on their own language. It allows them to think not only about their use of language in school but also in future roles as parents or at work.

## The Revised National Curriculum Programmes of Study

The changes in the National Curriculum in 2008 recognise the importance of creative approaches, not only in obvious places like poetry and storytelling, but also as part of analytical work. The Programmes of Study advocate 'inventive approaches', 'risk-taking' and experimentation as key ways of capturing students' interest and developing confident, knowledgeable and sophisticated users of language in a range of contexts and for a variety of purposes. *Language Works* offers opportunities for such open-ended, exploratory and creative work around language.

## What is Language Works?

10 units for students 11-16 (and in some cases beyond). The units include opportunities for students to:

- explore how language contributes to our identities as individuals and members of groups and communities
- discover more about accents, dialects and Standard English – their features, functions and attitudes to them
- investigate how language changes
- learn about key aspects of language – grammar, lexis, register and so on – in context and without overdosing on technical language
- find out how a baby learns language and what a parent can do to help
- explore the language of children's books and how children learn to read
- think about how groups use language to get things done, in the workplace and in their own classroom interactions
- learn about the differences between speech and writing
- develop their own skill as tellers of stories and writers of stories
- explore the language of 21st-century texts such as texts, emails and blogs.

## The Language Works DVD

If you're learning about language you need to watch and listen to examples of it in all its variety! Central to *Language Works* is the DVD which includes a rich collection of clips that form the basis of several of the units. The clips range from school students talking, to a baby's talk over eighteen months, from Jamie Oliver to *The Apprentice*, from *The Catherine Tate Show* to Courtney Pine on the origins of the word 'Cool'. There's Phil Jupitus on code-switching, Tony Blair, TV news broadcasters, children learning to read and more.

The DVD could be used by A Level Language teachers as a stand-alone resource, fuelling work on anything from language change, spoken language, accent and dialect to debates on prescriptivism and descriptivism.

# My Language

## Influences and Attitudes

# Teachers' Notes

## Teachers' Notes

### DVD Menu

The following activities have a DVD element signalled with this icon: **DVD**

| Selectable section | Duration | Onscreen title | See page |
|---|---|---|---|
| Voicing your opinion | 1 min 30 | | 13 |
| Teenagers talking | 5 mins | Family | 15 |
| | | Making judgements | |
| | | Adapting your speech | |
| What is accent/dialect? | 3 mins 45 | An expert view | 16 |
| | | Teenagers on dialect | |
| Talking posh (*The difference between Standard English and RP*) | 3 mins | An expert view | 17 |
| | | Channel 4 News | |
| | | ITV News | |
| Translating the news | 45 secs | | 18 |
| Language and belonging | 3 mins 15 | Tony Blair | 23 |
| | | Shifting your language | |
| | | Getting it wrong – *The Catherine Tate Show* | |

### Additional Resources

Worksheets, colour images, further resources in PDF format included on the DVD are signalled with this icon:

My Language

# My Language

**In this unit you will:**
- explore the way you use language
- learn about the difference between accent and dialect
- find out about Standard English and Received Pronunciation
- consider attitudes towards the way people speak.

## Starting to Think About Language – Voicing Your Opinion

People often feel very strongly about the way they speak and use language. Language has a close connection to the way we see ourselves. It is also one of the things that helps us feel like we belong to, or fit in with our family, friendship groups and the place we live or were born.

■ Read through the comments, opinions and views on the way people speak and use language on page 14. Choose two that you feel strongly about.

■ In pairs, talk about your chosen statements. Make a note of the key points to share in class discussion.

■ Take it in turns to read out your statements and your reasons for choosing them.

■ You are now going to listen to four adults and two teenagers talking about the way they speak. The first time you listen, focus on *the way* they speak, rather than what they say. Make a note of your response in the chart below.

■ Watch the clip again, this time listening to *what* each person says about the way they speak.

■ Share your responses in class discussion then, on your own, write two or three sentences summing up your own thoughts about the way people speak and use language.

|  | How the Person Speaks | What the Person Says |
|---|---|---|
| Brian Sewell, art critic |  |  |
| Jacob Rees Mogg, politician |  |  |
| Roger McGough, poet |  |  |
| John Cooper Clark, poet |  |  |
| Corey, Liverpool student |  |  |
| Stephen, Liverpool student |  |  |

© English and Media Centre, 2008

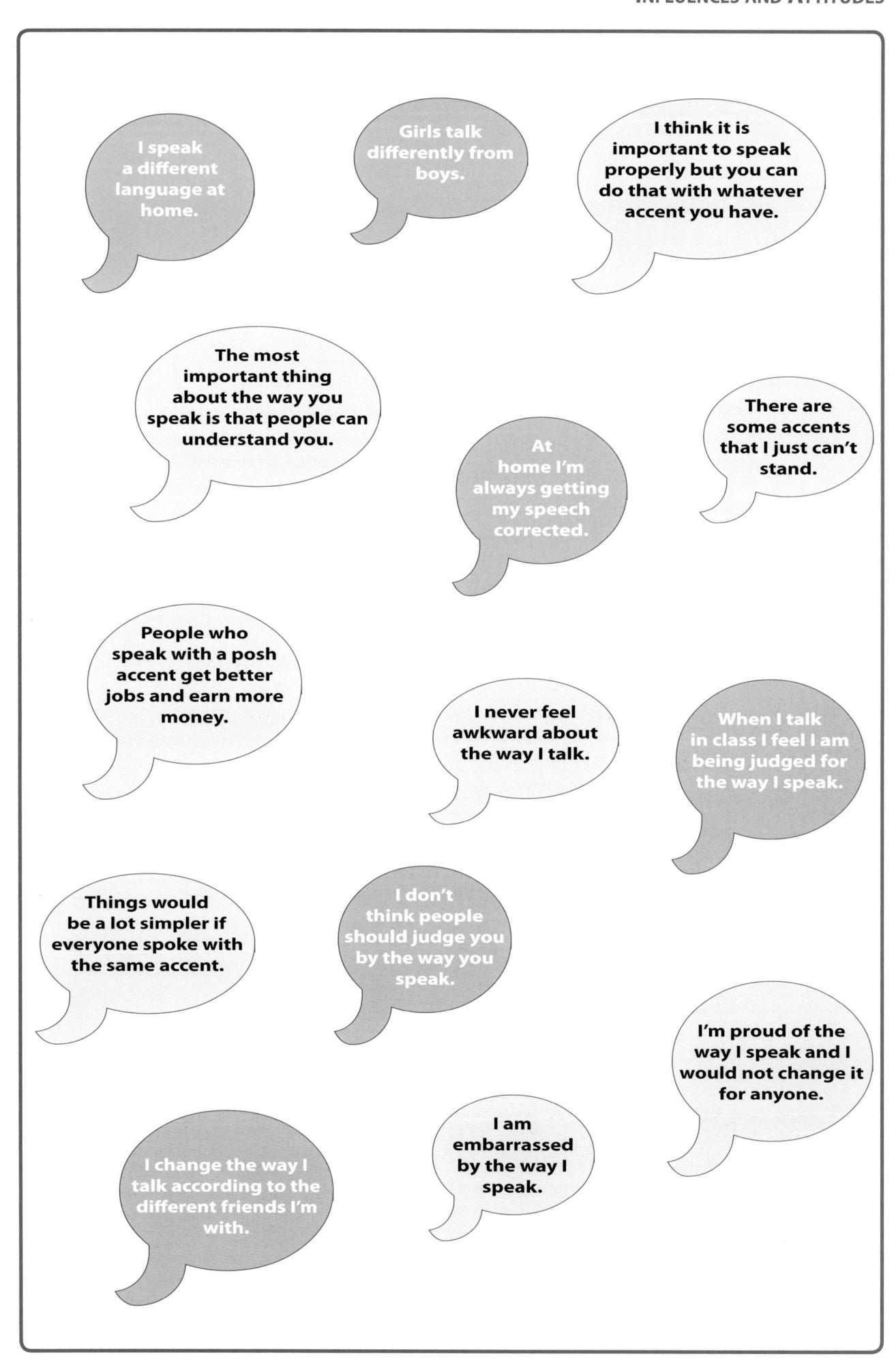

# INFLUENCES AND ATTITUDES

- I speak a different language at home.
- Girls talk differently from boys.
- I think it is important to speak properly but you can do that with whatever accent you have.
- The most important thing about the way you speak is that people can understand you.
- At home I'm always getting my speech corrected.
- There are some accents that I just can't stand.
- People who speak with a posh accent get better jobs and earn more money.
- I never feel awkward about the way I talk.
- When I talk in class I feel I am being judged for the way I speak.
- Things would be a lot simpler if everyone spoke with the same accent.
- I don't think people should judge you by the way you speak.
- I'm proud of the way I speak and I would not change it for anyone.
- I change the way I talk according to the different friends I'm with.
- I am embarrassed by the way I speak.

14  LANGUAGE WORKS  © English and Media Centre, 2008

MY LANGUAGE

### Teenagers Talking – Views and Attitudes

You are going to watch groups of students talking about the way they and other people speak.

■ After watching each section note down one or two points that particularly strike you, including any thoughts about your own language use.

**1. Family**

I was interested in ............................................................

............................................................................

Thoughts about *my* language use: ........................................

............................................................................

**2. Making judgements**

I was interested in ............................................................

............................................................................

Thoughts about *my* language use: ........................................

............................................................................

**3. Adapting your speech**

I was interested in ............................................................

............................................................................

Thoughts about *my* language use: ........................................

............................................................................

■ Share your responses in class discussion.

### Over to you – a mini-presentation

What are your views about the way you speak and use language? Are you proud or embarrassed when other people draw attention to the way you speak? Do you have strong feelings about your accent? Do you think the way someone speaks reflects the sort of person they are?

■ Prepare a 2-minute mini-presentations on your views.

■ Take it in turns to record your mini-presentations on video to create a class montage of opinions.

© English and Media Centre, 2008     LANGUAGE WORKS   **15**

INFLUENCES AND ATTITUDES

## What is Accent? What is Dialect?

**An Expert View**

The language expert Dr Graeme Trousdale researches the ways different people use language.

■ Watch Graeme explain the difference between **Accent** and **Dialect**.

■ Turn to your partner and, in your own words, explain the difference between accent and dialect. You could use examples from the way you speak to illustrate your definition.

**Teenagers on Dialect**

The students on the DVD were asked to introduce some of the words that are particular either to the area they come from or to their age group. These words are examples of the students' dialect.

■ Listen to the students talking about the dialect words they use. Do you use the same or similar words for any of the ideas they describe, for example showing off or bullying? Or do you use completely different words?

■ On your own, list any examples of dialect words you use, or come up with dialect versions of the Standard English words suggested in the chart below.

| Playing truant | Feeling cold | Feeling pleased | Attractive | Make fun of | Good | Bad |
|---|---|---|---|---|---|---|
|  |  |  |  |  |  |  |

■ Share your dialect words in class discussion and record them in the chart. Next to each dialect word, make a note of the number of people who:

- use the word regularly
- have heard or understand the word but don't use it themselves.

Can you work out whether the words are examples of:

- regional dialect (likely to be used by most people who have grown up, or lived in the region a long time, but less so by people who have recently moved to the area)
- youth dialect (likely to be used by people of a similar age, wherever they live)
- family language (particular words used by your family, which may have their origin in made-up or baby words)?

■ Visit http://www.bbc.co.uk/voices/results/wordmap/ to compare the dialect words used by students in your class with those submitted to the 'Voices' project, a nationwide survey of dialect and language use in 2005.

## MY LANGUAGE

### The Difference Between Standard English and Received Pronunciation

**An Expert View**

- Listen to the language expert Graeme Trousdale defining **Standard English** and **Received Pronunciation**, then, in your own words, explain the difference between the two.

    Standard English is .....

    Received Pronunciation is ....

- As a class talk about anything that surprises or interests you in what Graeme Trousdale says about Standard English and Received Pronunciation.

One of the things Graeme Trousdale points out is that Standard English can be spoken with *any* regional accent. He himself is a good example of someone who speaks Standard English with a northern accent. Nowadays, television newsreaders speak with a variety of regional accents but all use Standard English.

- Watch the DVD clip to hear examples of Standard English being spoken first with Received Pronunciation and then with a regional accent.

    1) Standard English with Received Pronunciation: Jon Snow and Krishnan Guru-Murthy, Channel 4 News

    2) Standard English with a northern Irish accent: Bill Neely, ITN News.

### So What is Standard English?

Standard English is really a particular dialect of English. It was originally spoken in the East Midlands and south of the country, including the three important areas of Oxford, Cambridge and London. But it is the dialect which has come to be accepted as the national language. It's the vocabulary and grammar of Standard English which is taught in schools and which you use in writing. In speech you probably move between Standard and dialect forms of English, without even realising it. Sometimes it's the **words** that are different in a dialect (see page 16); sometimes it's the **grammar.**

- Here are some examples of expressions in Standard and non-Standard English grammar. Can you come up with any more examples?

| Standard English | Non-Standard (dialect) English |
|---|---|
| I don't want any. | I don't want none. |
| She talks nicely. | She talks nice. |
| We were only joking. I wasn't serious. | We was only joking. I weren't serious. |
| Next to those houses. | Next to them houses. |
| I already know who I want to marry. | Me know who me want to marry already. |
|  |  |
|  |  |

© English and Media Centre, 2008    LANGUAGE WORKS    **17**

## INFLUENCES AND ATTITUDES

### Translating the News

- Watch the newsreader Huw Edwards read the news. He's speaking Standard English with a Welsh accent.

- Read the transcript of the news item reprinted here. As a class, talk about the features which identify it as Standard English, for example correct verb forms such as 'has been greeted'. Mark these onto your transcript.

- In pairs, try 'translating' this news story from Standard English into your own regional dialect, for example: 'Na then? Y'alreet? Malcolm Glazer, th' rich yank's ony gone and tekken o'er United and't lads are creating'. If you don't speak a regional dialect, then you could try translating it into youth dialect.

> Good evening. Manchester United, the world's richest football club, has been taken over by the American businessman Malcolm Glazer. The news has been greeted with dismay and anger by many of the fans who've been protesting this evening claiming that Mr Glazer has no emotional attachment to the club. Mr Glazer has suddenly built up a controlling interest in United after months of manoeuvring. For the latest we can join Andy Parsons at Old Trafford.

- Annotate your news story to show the dialect features you have used.

- Take it in turns to read aloud your news stories and share your responses as a class. Does the news have a different meaning or impact on you when spoken in your dialect? How do you think people familiar with another regional dialect might respond?

- Use what you have discovered through this exercise to think about the two opinions in the chart below. Can you think of at least one point in favour and one point against each opinion?

| Opinion | Argument in Favour | Argument Against |
|---|---|---|
| It would be better if everyone used Standard English in speech as well as writing. | | |
| Dialects are a vital part of what makes English a living language and should be accepted in speech and writing. | | |

- Individually, write a statement summing up your own opinion of Standard English and whether or not it is something we should all be taught to speak and write.

MY LANGUAGE

### Standard English – the Great Debate

For this activity, you will work first in groups preparing your arguments, then join together as a class to perform the simulation.

**The Situation**

The Headteacher of your school is proposing that Standard English no longer be taught in speech or writing. All lessons will be taught using the local regional dialect. A public meeting has been called to discuss the proposal.

**The Roles**

The cards on page 20 summarise the opinions of the people who have asked to speak at the meeting. Your teacher will tell you which role your group should prepare.

**Preparing Your Argument**

- In your role-card group, brainstorm as many arguments as you can to support the opinion you have been given.

- Work together to draft an opening statement, summing up your arguments. Use what you know about speaking to argue and persuade to come up with some convincing ways of presenting your opinion.

- Look through your arguments and think about how people with a different opinion might argue against you. Make notes on how you could answer their objections and any further points you might want to make in the general discussion.

**The Public Debate**

- Your teacher will play the part of the Headteacher who will chair the discussion. One person from each group will be asked to present an opening statement. The rest of the class, acting in role, will be able to ask questions, raise objections or put forward arguments.

### Your Views

- Re-read the statement you wrote about your own views on Standard English before taking part in the 'Great Debate' role-play (see page 20). Has your opinion been altered by the opinions you put forward in role, or the other arguments you heard? If so, re-draft your statement to reflect your views now. If not, use what you have learned to develop your argument more fully.

## INFLUENCES AND ATTITUDES

### Parent (1)
You are concerned that your child will be at a disadvantage in exams if they are not taught Standard English.

### Student (1)
You don't think the school has a right to interfere in the way you speak.

### History teacher
You are frustrated by your students who don't seem able to write 'correct' English.

### Parent (2)
You are proud of your dialect and think the Headteacher is right in refusing to teach Standard English.

### Local employer
You think it is vital that people can use Standard English when required.

### Local Councillor
You think the Headteacher is doing the right thing in promoting the regional dialect.

### Student (2)
You are worried you will not get a good job if you cannot speak and write Standard English.

### English teacher
You think students should be taught about all different varieties of English, including Standard English.

### Student (3)
You have just started at this school, having moved from another part of the country.

MY LANGUAGE

## Language and Belonging

The politician Jacob Rees Mogg spoke about how difficult it would be to change his Received Pronunciation accent – and the fact he wouldn't want to, even to make himself more popular.

> I've always spoken in the way I've spoken. I've never tried to adopt a particular accent. Perhaps I should. Perhaps it would be better if I could model myself on Tony Blair and drop all my 'ts' at the end of words but I think I'd find it very irritating.
>
> *Jacob Rees Mogg, politician*

Some of the students you listened to also said they would not change their accent or dialect, even if other people teased them for it:

> Why change your accent? It's nothing really, just the way you talk.
>
> *Patrick, Liverpool student*

> I wouldn't change my accent for no-one. You shouldn't be like a lap dog and if people say change your accent, you shouldn't try and change your accent. You should be proud of your accent.
>
> *Stephen, Liverpool student*

Some of the students did think there might be times when they might change their accent.

> If I go to a fancy restaurant and all that, I'll probably change cos I'll be like 'Oh pardon' and like 'thank you' and all that instead of like 'ta'. So that's when I change it in restaurants. Otherwise I'll just keep the way I am.
>
> *Ashley, Liverpool student*

The poet John Cooper Clarke talked about how, when he was growing up, everyone knew there were times and situations when you would need to speak Standard English.

> It was just taken as read then, you know, there was a proper way to speak. You know, nobody had a problem with it, it wasn't seen as some big conspiracy to try and make us all you know, the same. There was no ideas of conformity. It was just accepted. It was alright to talk like this but you'd never get a job with ITN.
>
> *John Cooper Clarke, poet*

### A Language Continuum Line (see page 22)

What about you? Do you change the way you speak in different situations? Are there times when you pronounce your words more clearly, or speak the sort of English you would normally use just in writing? Are there times when you deliberately speak with a stronger accent or use more dialect words or expressions?

- In pairs, look at the situations listed on page 22 and, for each one, think about the way you speak and use language. Decide where you would place each situation on the continuum line.

- Feed back your decisions in class discussion and talk about any patterns you notice. (For example, when do people speak most informally or use most dialect words and expressions?)

**INFLUENCES AND ATTITUDES**

## A Language Continuum Line

**I speak with a strong accent.
I use dialect grammar.
I use dialect words.
I use slang.**

**I speak clearly.
I use Standard grammar.
I do not use dialect words.
I do not use slang.**

- Class discussion
- Explaining to a teacher why I'm late
- Job or college interview
- Speaking to someone I don't know on the phone
- Meeting new people of my age
- Chatting to a parent or carer
- Doing a talk for a speaking and listening assessment
- Talking to friends on a mobile phone
- Speaking to a brother or sister

22   LANGUAGE WORKS   © English and Media Centre, 2008

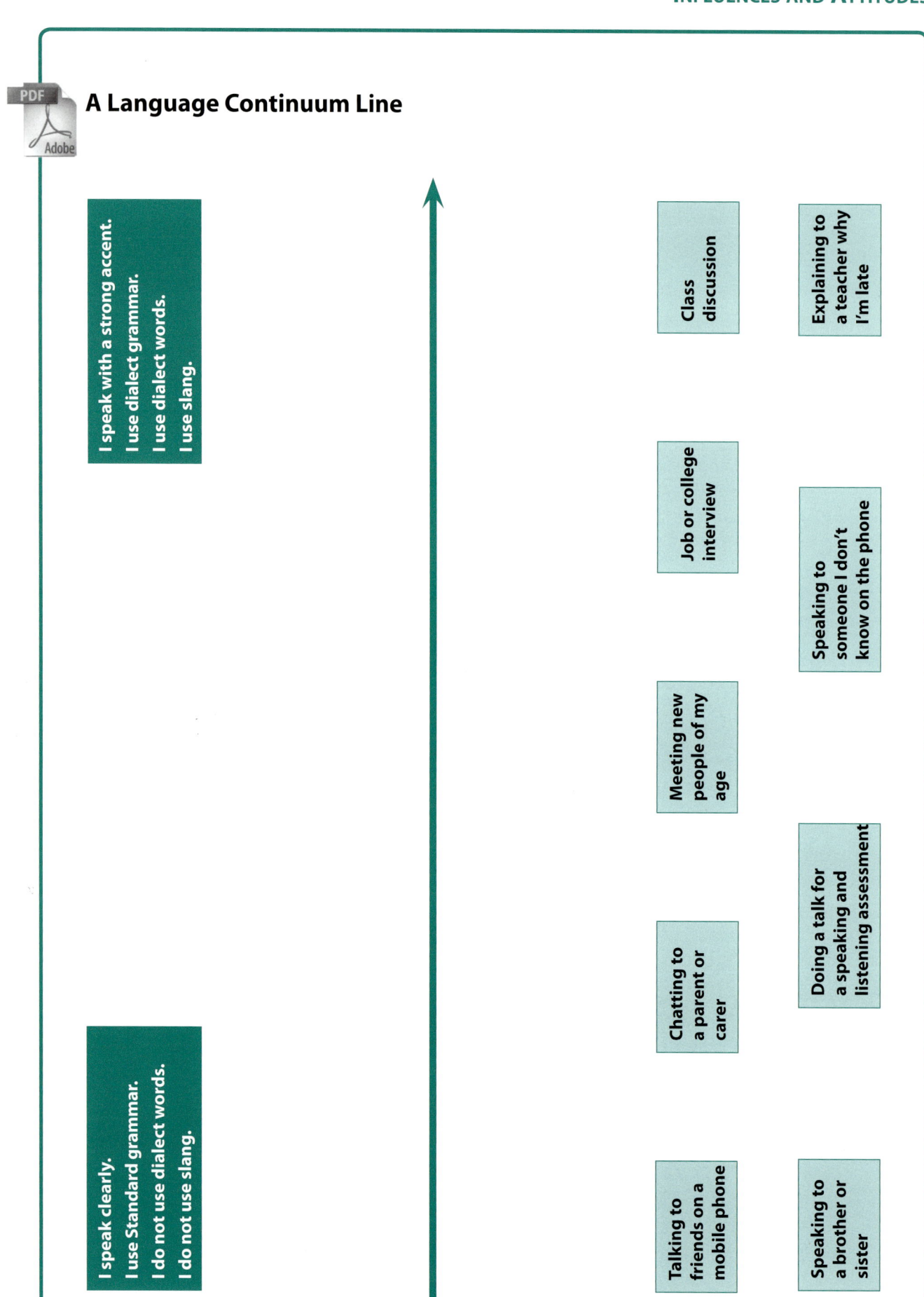

## My Language

### Language and Belonging (continued)

This section of the DVD includes three separate clips. Pause between each one so that you can complete the activities.

**Tony Blair Talking**

In this DVD clip Tony Blair is shown speaking on three different occasions.

- Make notes on what you notice about the way he speaks on each occasion.

- Feed back what you notice in class discussion. Why do you think he might have changed the way he speaks?

|   | What I Noticed |
|---|---|
| 1 |  |
| 2 |  |
| 3 |  |

**Shifting Your Language – Phil Jupitus**

Sometimes people adapt their speech depending on the situation they are in and who they are talking to.

- Watch the comedian Phil Jupitus describing a man changing the way he speaks within the same conversation.

- What does this story tell you about the way people change the way they speak according to who they are with? Share your ideas in class discussion.

**Getting it Wrong – The Catherine Tate Show**

Language plays an important part in feeling part of a group, of fitting in, of being accepted. Get it wrong and you risk being made fun of or even being left out of the group.

You are now going to watch a sketch by the comedian Catherine Tate. In it Lauren tries out the latest 'cool' word on two of her friends.

- Watch the sketch and talk about the humour of the situation.

- What does it tell you about the role language plays in being accepted into the 'right' friendship groups? How does this relate to *your* experiences?

© English and Media Centre, 2008    LANGUAGE WORKS

## INFLUENCES AND ATTITUDES

### Your Unique Language – Where Does it Come From?

Every individual – even in the same family – has their own personal language. Your language is as unique to you as your fingerprints. Language experts call this individual language your **idiolect**. Listed here are a few of the influences shaping the way you use language:

- where you live
- your family background
- television programmes from around the world
- hobbies
- friends.

The poet Michael Rosen presents a radio programme exploring the way we use language. Here he explores what has influenced his personal language (idiolect).

■ In pairs, read Michael Rosen's account, highlighting or underlining all the influences on his idiolect. The first one has been done for you.

> Here's me: I learnt my main, basic language, English, from <u>my parents and my brother.</u> I also speak quite good French which I learnt from my father, many holidays in France and school. Same goes for German, but much less well. But there's another language, or part of a language: Yiddish. That's the language that was spoken by Eastern European Jews. There are many, perhaps hundreds of Yiddish words and phrases that I know. They came to me mostly from my parents and my mother's parents but were confirmed by knowing other Jewish people here and in America: 'shlump', 'chutzpah', 'shmerel', 'in shtuch' and so on.
>
> There are specific phrases, expressions, jokes, quotes from plays, catch-phrases, rude and jokey ways of twisting the language and the like that I can trace to individuals: 'you must be out of your mind' – my father; calling the broken dishwasher 'the wishdasher' – my mother. At school in North West London there were games and rituals which are called different things elsewhere: 'he', 'kingie', 'fainites', 'dobbing' for 'it'. 'Dets' were school detentions. When my own children use different words I have to ignore mine.
>
> Some of our language comes to us as a result of education: there are the schooling words like 'subjects', 'invigilation', 'Year 9 SATs'. In my day there were 'O levels'. There are academic words like: 'quadratic equation', 'metaphor' and the like. The odd bit of literature might have rubbed off on you – anything from Roald Dahl's 'snozzcumbers' to Shakespeare's 'whirligig of time'. For brief periods I find myself using catch-phrases I hear from TV like the 'waassuuuuup' from the Budweiser ad, and some of Harry Enfield's lines. You may not know it but, thanks to your parents and grandparents, you might use old catch-phrases from previous eras, like 'Nice one, Cyril!'
>
> But what about my dialects and accents? My main voice is what used to be called 'suburban cockney' but is now called 'Estuary English'. This comes from my school friends. My main dialect I would identify as informal standard English. Unlike my children, I don't say 'ain't', 'we was' and 'he come through the door'. But I do say, 'Me and Joe were in the car'. When I'm broadcasting, I know that I tend to formalise my dialect – ('Joe and I...'), and switch the accent from Estuary to 'Received Pronunciation'.

My Language

### A Pie Chart of Your Personal Language (Idiolect)

What about you? Where does your language come from?

- In pairs or small groups, talk about all the different people, places, programmes and so on that you think have shaped the way you use language.

- Working on your own, draw a pie chart to estimate how important each of these possible influences has been in shaping the way you use language.

- In each segment of pie write down a few examples of the words and expressions you've taken from that influence. Below is an example of one person's pie chart to show you the sort of thing you might do.

- Compare your pie chart with one or two other people in your class.

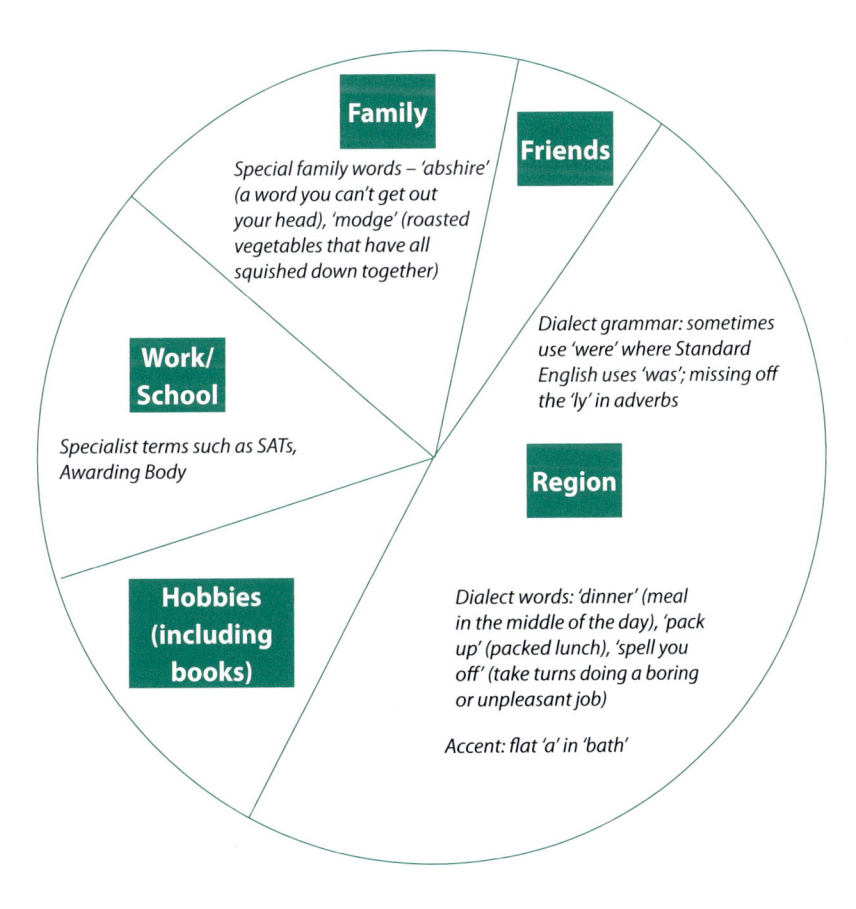

**Family**
*Special family words – 'abshire' (a word you can't get out your head), 'modge' (roasted vegetables that have all squished down together)*

**Friends**

*Dialect grammar: sometimes use 'were' where Standard English uses 'was'; missing off the 'ly' in adverbs*

**Work/School**
*Specialist terms such as SATs, Awarding Body*

**Region**
*Dialect words: 'dinner' (meal in the middle of the day), 'pack up' (packed lunch), 'spell you off' (take turns doing a boring or unpleasant job)*

*Accent: flat 'a' in 'bath'*

**Hobbies (including books)**

© English and Media Centre, 2008

LANGUAGE WORKS

**25**

# INFLUENCES AND ATTITUDES

# Extension Activities

## A Day in My Language Life

As well as exploring his idiolect, Michael Rosen has explored the different ways he uses language during a single day.

- As a class, read the extract from 'A Day in the Language Life of Michael Rosen'.

- In pairs, find examples of the different ways Michael Rosen uses language throughout the day and fill in the second column of the chart.

| Language Use | Examples |
| --- | --- |
| To give or get information | |
| To share ideas | |
| To chat, to be sociable | |
| For play | |
| To plan or think | |
| To get things done | |
| To tell stories | |
| To joke | |
| To keep a record of things | |

## A Day in the Language Life of Michael Rosen

I get up and creep about the house really early not talking to anyone because I have to get a cab. This means checking what is known in the entertainment business as a 'call sheet'. This is like a timetable, with people's telephone numbers on it. It also has the code I have to use to get my tickets out of a machine on Paddington station. So this is a mix of names, numbers, times and codes. There's nothing there to do with emotions and feelings, nothing to do with ideas. Every letter and number has to be exactly right or I will turn up at the wrong place or at the wrong time, or press the wrong buttons on a machine. If any of that happens, the work of a whole day will go wrong and the radio programme I'm supposed to make, won't get made.

The cab arrives and very soon I'm having a conversation with the cabby. He's a Greek Cypriot about the same age as me (that's nearly 60), and we're soon talking about our adult sons. He tells me a story about how his son moved out but he, the cabby, comes home one night and his wife is ironing

## My Language

some shirts. He asks whose shirts they are and she says they belong to their son. He tells me he couldn't believe it. 'He's nearly thirty, he's moved out and she's ironing his shirts!' He tells me he rang his son, got him over, bundled the shirts into a suitcase and told him to get out. I tell a story about my son living in what used to be my office at the end of our garden.

Then I get to Paddington, we tell each other to have a good day with a kind of ironic laugh, as if it's not possible to have a good day. I tap in the code, get my tickets, and read the tickets and signs very closely to make sure I get on the right train.

On the train, I do the crossword and check over my script. I try to do what's known as a cryptic crossword. This is, in a way, similar to the accurate language of timetables, except that everything is in a code that I have to unlock. This is language as a game.

Then I look at the script I'll be reading today. This is full of jargon and in-group language. Things like, 'WOM6', meaning Word of Mouth (that's the programme I present, and it's the sixth one in a series of 8). It talks of 'items' – which to listeners means five or six conversations on a topic. It says 'clip' meaning a recording of music or speech that will come before or after I've said something. It says, 'IN', 'OUT', and 'DUR'. But there's nothing next to these words. 'IN' will be the person's opening words, 'OUT' will be their last words and 'DUR' is how long the whole clip will last. It stands for 'Duration'.

I start to scribble all over the bits of paper, coming up with ideas for me to say. I'm revising, re-jigging and editing. There are also some questions that I'm going to be asking a famous etymologist (someone who knows about the origins of words). I start thinking about the questions. I'm using language to plan.

Then, it's out of the train at Bristol (after listening to the various announcements about 'tea, coffee, light refreshments and snacks, apologies for the late arrival of this train').

Once I arrive at Bristol and meet up with the team of people working on Word of Mouth, we begin with a bit of mild joshing. Stuff about football, weather, cabs, TV last night. I get into the studio and there's a lot of technical stuff about 'lines to London', 'faders', 'howlround', 'echo', 'compression', 'popping' and then we get through to the man I'm interviewing.

### My Language Life

■ You are now going to list some of the different types of language *you* use during the day, using the chart on page 28 to record your discoveries.

- Choose five points in the day, for example, breakfast or walking home from school. Write these in column 1.
- In column 2, note down where you were and who else was with you.
- In column 3 record all the different ways in which you used language. For example reading a magazine at breakfast, talking to your friends at break, listening to your teachers, emailing and so on.
- In column 4 write down an example of each different type of language use.

■ Use the information on your chart to write your own 'A Day in my Language Life'.

**INFLUENCES AND ATTITUDES**

## A Day in My Language Life

| My Day | Where? Who With? | Language Use | An Example |
|--------|------------------|--------------|------------|
|        |                  |              |            |
|        |                  |              |            |

**TELLING A STORY**

# TELLING A STORY
## FROM TALK TO TEXT

# Teachers' Notes

## Options

In this unit there are two different stories to choose from. The activities are exactly the same. The choice of story is to give you different options depending on the age and interests of your class.

## DVD Menu

The DVD clips are signalled with this icon: **DVD**

| Selectable section | Duration | Onscreen title | See page |
|---|---|---|---|
| Sevim's story | 50 secs | | 33 |
| Tim's story | 50 secs | | 38 |

## Additional Resources

Worksheets, colour images, further resources in PDF format included on the DVD are signalled with this icon:

**TELLING A STORY**

# Telling a Story

**In this unit you will:**
- tell a story
- think about the way you tell stories
- compare spoken and written stories
- learn about the different features of speech and writing.

## Stories You Tell

Everyone tells stories. Here are some examples of the kinds of stories people tell:

- 'the story' of what happened at school or work each day
- funny, horrible, shocking or frightening things that have happened to you, told to a friend
- stories in the news
- what's been happening in a soap opera or TV drama
- things other people have told you about
- stories you've read and liked.

■ What kinds of stories do you tell? Make a chart like the one below and fill it in to show the kinds of stories you tell.

■ Compare your chart with those of two or three other people in your class.

| I tell stories about: | A lot | Sometimes | Never |
|---|---|---|---|
| My family | | | |
| My friends | | | |
| Arguments or fights | | | |
| Funny things | | | |
| Accidents and injuries | | | |
| School | | | |
| Soap operas | | | |
| Childhood memories | | | |
| Something strange or mysterious | | | |
| The story of a book I've read | | | |

© English and Media Centre, 2008     LANGUAGE WORKS

# From Talk to Text

## Spoken Stories

### Telling Anecdotes

One kind of spoken story is called an **anecdote**. It's a little story of something that has happened to you or someone you know.

■ In this activity you are going to tell an anecdote to a partner.

- Pick one of the topic areas from the chart on page 31.
- Think of a little story you could tell of something that has happened to you. It could be something that happened recently, or a memory of something from the past.
- Without pausing to think too much, tell your story to your partner. (Partners can react, ask questions or comment if you want to!)
- Now change roles so that the other person has a chance to tell their story.
- If you think your partner told a really good story, perhaps he/she might be willing to tell it to the whole class? Listen to a few of the stories as a whole class, then share your ideas about what makes a good spoken story.

### Talking About the Stories

As a whole class, talk about the stories you've told and heard, both in your pairs and the ones the class heard. Here are some things to think about:

- How much repetition and back-tracking was there?
- What did gestures, facial expressions, body language add to the story?
- Were there hesitations?
- Were there lots of fillers, such as 'er' and 'um'?
- How important was tone of voice?
- How were the stories introduced?
- How did the story end?

■ What did you notice about the way you told your stories? Were there any patterns across all the stories?

**TELLING A STORY**

# Option 1 – Sevim's Story

## Sevim's Spoken Story

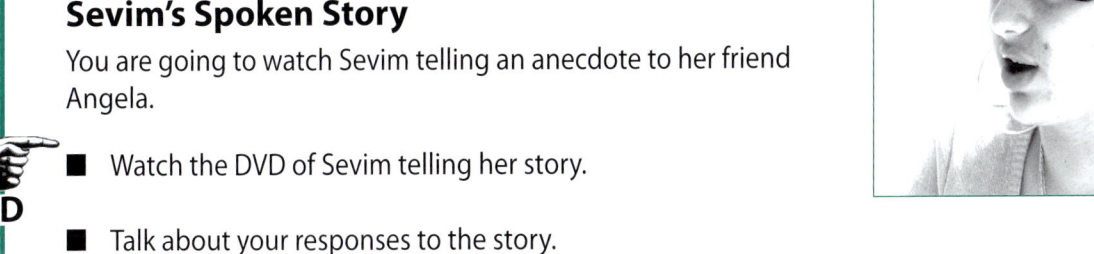

You are going to watch Sevim telling an anecdote to her friend Angela.

- Watch the DVD of Sevim telling her story.

- Talk about your responses to the story.

- Watch the DVD clip a second time. This time you are going to try to analyse more closely the way she tells the story, using this chart to help you. Make a note of anything you notice, for instance you might comment on the way Sevim's lively tone of voice made you want to listen to her story.

| Repetition and back-tracking | |
|---|---|
| Gestures, facial expressions and body language | |
| Hesitations (ums and ers) | |
| Fillers (sort of, y'know etc) | |
| Tone of voice | |
| Introducing the story | |
| Ending the story | |

The transcript of Sevim's story is included on page 34. Very short pauses are shown with the symbol (.). Longer pauses are shown with the number of seconds in the brackets, for example (2) shows a pause of 2 seconds.

- Use the transcript to identify anything more about the way she tells her anecdote, for instance:

    – As a written text what makes the transcript difficult to read?

    – What makes the spoken story enjoyable?

    – How does Sevim engage her listener when she is telling her story?

OK (.) I think I was 7 (.) and me my friend and her mum went to the park and (.) I don't know if you know if but this thing you hold on to it and you slide across and then it bounces and then it comes back and you just, just like a little hole thing that you just slide across it (.) OK OK she had her go and her mum asked me if I wanted a go and I said no (.) but (.) then (1) [*laughs*] I got on it and she pushed me and I got to the end and cos it I was going so fast it didn't come back I couldn't even hold on (.) so I went it I just let go couldn't even hold on so I let go went flying into the air yeh landed on my elbows cracked this bone and dislocated the other one (1) and I couldn't even see properly and I had like to go home holding onto her mum because couldn't see or anything (2.5) yep (2) really really bad I know

**TELLING A STORY**

## Sevim's Story in Writing

Sevim went on to write up her anecdote as a written story.

■ Read Sevim's written version on page 36 and talk about what you thought of it. For example what did you enjoy and why?

■ Now go on to explore the differences between the written version and the spoken one by looking at the two side by side (page 37) and coming up with a list of differences. Here are a few ideas to get you started:

*The spoken story shows you things using gestures.*

*The written story describes things in words.*

■ Look at this list of the typical features of speech and writing:

| Speech | Writing |
| --- | --- |
| Is normally spontaneous, not planned | Is planned |
| Can't be revised | Can be re-drafted |
| Is only listened to once (unless recorded) | Can be re-read |
| Is addressed to someone who is there, face-to-face | Is addressed to someone who probably isn't there, and isn't necessarily known |
| Makes use of body language, gestures, pace and tone of voice | Uses paragraphing, capital letters, exclamation marks, underlining and so on to suggest tone of voice etc. |
| Often involves feedback (laughter, nodding, clapping etc.) and interruptions | If there is feedback, it's not immediate |
| Less rigidly organised | More organised, following certain rules depending on the kind of writing |
| Is often more informal and uses language to match the listener(s), such as slang, in-jokes, personal language | Is often more formal and removes in-jokes and personal language, so that it can be understood by anyone |
| Refers to things in the present situation, using words like 'here', 'that', 'this', 'over there' that the listener can see or understand without explanation | Has to explain everything about the context, because the reader doesn't know anything about the situation |

■ Look back at the transcript of Sevim's spoken story and the written version. See if you now want to add anything to your list of differences, based on the new ideas you've come across.

© English and Media Centre, 2008      LANGUAGE WORKS

## Cracking Fun!

It was the same as usual, I'd done nothing differently. Same cereal. Same hairstyle. Same skip off the last step. They say 'expect the unexpected'. If only a 7-year-old knew how! Bored out of my mind, I went to my friend's house, Sophie. She lived two doors away, wasn't particularly fun, but anything would be better than doing nothing at home alone, listening to that boring song called silence. Sophie's house would be less boring, is what I thought. Correction, wrongly thought. Everybody has the friend they only spend time with because there's nothing better to do, and because they're always there. She decided she wanted to go to the park. I didn't think we would be long, so I didn't tell my grandmother, and besides, her mother was coming with us.

Mistake number one: going to the park. We got to the park and the shiny blue climbing frame caught Sophie's eye. It drew her in like a sweaty old man to a free sample of Coke Zero. Quiet little me hesitantly followed her. I really didn't want to have a go – I could tell that that thing was a danger hazard from a mile off. She swung on it like a chimp. A chimp whose back I'd now like to pluck every single hair off. Her mother asked if I wanted to have a go. I politely declined, as I didn't want to be pushed to my death, thanks. After a while of Sophie's begging and pleading and variations of 'Aww but it's really fun, Sev!!' I gave in.

Mistake number two: giving in. It would have been more fun to stay at home and roll down the stairs. Backwards. With a kitchen knife behind my ear. Her mother lifted me up so I could hold onto the sliding handle. I held on for dear life, legs dangling and eyes wide. Just as I was ready to happily slide along, Sophie appeared from nowhere and pushed me with all of her might. It went all too quickly. I don't remember sliding happily along like I had planned to. I do remember however, flying into the air, doing a one hundred and eighty degrees mid-flight flip and landing on both elbows, smashing my right arm. Nice.

I couldn't see very well, figures were disguised by a monster of a blur. It was like trying to watch a programme on television when the channel isn't tuned in properly. An ugly grey fuzz that is adamant on staying. An unwanted guest with a smelly dog in a five star hotel. I had to walk home stuck to her mother's side because I could barely walk straight. I dreaded telling my grandmother. Not only did I avoid asking for permission to go to the park, nor did I ask for permission for whether or not I could go home with a cracked right radius and a dislocated left arm.

Tears created a dream-like film, and that evening I went to Homerton Hospital where they gave me an ugly sickly pink sponge sling. Sophie apologised and they say sorry seems to be the hardest word, but sometimes 'sorry' is even harder to *accept*. You'd think at school they would at least give a child less work to do, but no Sir, school was the same as usual.

## TELLING A STORY

| Transcript | Written Story |
|---|---|
| OK (.) I think I was 7 (.) and me my friend and her mum went to the park and (.) I don't know if you know if but this thing you hold on to it and you slide across and then it bounces and then it comes back and you just, just like a little hole thing that you just slide across it (.) OK OK she had her go and her mum asked me if I wanted a go and I said no (.) but (.) then (1) (laughs) I got on it and she pushed me and I got to the end and cos it I was going so fast it didn't come back I couldn't even hold on (.) so I went it I just let go couldn't even hold on so I let go went flying into the air yeh landed on my elbows cracked this bone and dislocated the other one (1) and I couldn't even see properly and I had like to go home holding onto her mum because couldn't see or anything (2.5) yep (2) really really bad I know | Cracking Fun! <br><br> It was the same as usual, I'd done nothing differently. Same cereal. Same hairstyle. Same skip off the last step. They say 'expect the unexpected'. If only a 7-year-old knew how! Bored out of my mind, I went to my friends house, Sophie. She lived two doors away, wasn't particularly fun, but anything would be better than doing nothing at home alone, listening to that boring song called silence. Sophie's house would be less boring, is what I thought. Correction, wrongly thought. Everybody has the friend they only spend time with because there's nothing better to do, and because they're always there. She decided she wanted to go to the park. I didn't think we would be long, so I didn't tell my grandmother, and besides, her mother was coming with us. <br><br> Mistake number one: going to the park. We got to the park and the shiny blue climbing frame caught Sophie's eye. It drew her in like a sweaty old man to a free sample of Coke Zero. Quiet little me hesitantly followed her. I really didn't want to have a go – I could tell that that thing was a danger hazard from a mile off. She swung on it like a chimp. A chimp whose back I'd now like to pluck every single hair off. Her mother asked if I wanted to have a go. I politely declined, as I didn't want to be pushed to my death, thanks. After a while of Sophie's begging and pleading and variations of 'Aww but it's really fun, Sev!!' I gave in. <br><br> Mistake number two: giving in. It would have been more fun to stay at home and roll down the stairs. Backwards. With a kitchen knife behind my ear. Her mother lifted me up so I could hold onto the sliding handle. I held on for dear life, legs dangling and eyes wide. Just as I was ready to happily slide along, Sophie appeared from nowhere and pushed me with all of her might. It went all too quickly. I don't remember sliding happily along like I had planned to. I do remember however, flying into the air, doing a one hundred and eighty degrees mid flight flip and landing on both elbows, smashing my right arm. Nice. <br><br> I couldn't see very well, figures were disguised by a monster of a blur. It was like trying to watch a programme on television when the channel isn't tuned in properly. An ugly grey fuzz, that is adamant on staying. An unwanted guest with a smelly dog in a five star hotel. I had to walk home stuck to her mother's side because I could barely walk straight. I dreaded telling my grandmother. Not only did I avoid asking for permission to go to the park, nor did I ask for permission for whether or not I could go home with a cracked right radius and a dislocated left arm. <br><br> Tears created a dream-like film, and that evening I went to Homerton Hospital where they gave me an ugly sickly pink sponge sling. Sophie apologised and they say sorry seems to be the hardest word, but sometimes 'sorry' is even harder to *accept*. You'd think at school they would at least give a child less work to do, but no Sir, school was the same as usual. |

FROM TALK TO TEXT

## Option 2 – Tim's story

### Tim's Spoken Story

You are going to watch Tim telling an anecdote to his friend Naq.

- Watch the DVD of Tim telling his story.

- Talk about your response to his story.

- Look at it a second time. This time you are going to try to analyse more closely the way he tells the story, using this chart to help you. Jot down anything you notice, then share your ideas as a whole class.

| Repetition and back-tracking | |
|---|---|
| Gestures, facial expressions and body language | |
| Hesitations (ums and ers) | |
| Fillers (sort of, y'know etc.) | |
| Tone of voice | |
| Introducing the story | |
| Ending the story | |

The transcript of Tim's story is included on page 39. Very short pauses are shown with the symbol (.). Longer pauses are shown with the number of seconds in the brackets, for example (2) shows a pause of 2 seconds.

- Use the transcript to identify anything more about the way Tim tells his anecdote, for instance:
    - As a written text what makes the transcript difficult to read?
    - What makes spoken story enjoyable?
    - How does Tim engage his listener when he is telling his story?

## TELLING A STORY

Let me think (.) it was like (.) year 1 just after

Reception (1) and I wasn't used to not being

in the nursery part of the school (.) and

then I remember as I was being taken to my

classroom I remember I just burst into tears (.)

I was just going mad because (.) like (.) I think

something silly like (.) my name wasn't on my

normal peg (.) where I put my coat so then I

was just like (1) like in hysteric tears was just

really like (1) annoyed at everything (1) so yes

(1) I had all the teachers trying to calm me

down like they do in primary school calm me

down be nice (.) I just wasn't having it (.) I was

just really upset

FROM TALK TO TEXT

## Tim's Story in Writing

Tim went on to write up his anecdote as a written story.

- Read Tim's written version on page 41 and talk about what you thought of it. For example what did you enjoy and why?

- Now go on to explore the differences between the written version and the spoken one by putting the two side by side (page 42) and coming up with a list of differences. Here are a few ideas to get you started:

    *The spoken story shows you things using gestures.*

    *The written story describes things in words.*

- Look at this list of the typical features of speech and writing:

| Speech | Writing |
| --- | --- |
| Is normally spontaneous, not planned | Is planned |
| Can't be revised | Can be re-drafted |
| Is only listened to once (unless recorded) | Can be re-read |
| Is addressed to someone who is there, face-to-face | Is addressed to someone who probably isn't there, and isn't necessarily known |
| Makes use of body language, gestures, pace and tone of voice | Uses paragraphing, capital letters, exclamation marks, underlining and so on to suggest tone of voice etc. |
| Often involves feedback (laughter, nodding, clapping etc.) and interruptions | If there is feedback, it's not immediate |
| Less rigidly organised | More organised, following certain rules depending on the kind of writing |
| Is often more informal and uses language to match the listener(s), such as slang, in-jokes, personal language | Is often more formal and removes in-jokes and personal language, so that it can be understood by anyone |
| Refers to things in the present situation, using words like 'here', 'that', 'this', 'over there' that the listener can see or understand without explanation | Has to explain everything about the context, because the reader doesn't know anything about the situation |

- Look back at the transcripts of Tim's spoken and written stories. See if you now want to add anything to your list of differences, based on the new ideas you've come across.

**40**  LANGUAGE WORKS © English and Media Centre, 2008

## TELLING A STORY

**First Day Of School**

When you are young, you never think you will grow up and everything seems to be perfect and you know no different. However, change when you're young can be quite difficult to comprehend, as I experienced.

It was in 1995 and the previous year I had been perfectly happy in nursery. So when my mum took me into school, a horrible surprise hit me when she was leading me somewhere other than nursery. I was being taken away from my sand pits, tiny bicycles and toy cars and over to the big, grey and dull prison which was primary school. Once the fact that I was not going to be in nursery anymore set in, I exploded into hysterical tears. I was uncontrollable and kept storming off, with my mum and teachers having to keep dragging me back.

My mum then calmed me down and told me that everything would be alright and I was all smiles again.

However, when I realised that my coat peg wouldn't be in the same place, this again set me off into hysterics. I was inconsolable at this point and it took my mum and teachers ages to calm me down. However, I think I just realised that I wouldn't get my own way and when I went into my new classroom, I was again happy and from then on, my primary school days were very happy.

Looking back on it now, I can understand why I may have been so upset. Unexpected change can shake even adults and for me it took me by complete surprise. My brain just couldn't understand why everyone was making me leave nursery and I was just a very angry 5-year-old.

# From Talk to Text

| Transcript | Written Story |
|---|---|
| Let me think (.) it was like (.) year 1 just after Reception (1) and I wasn't used to not being in the nursery part of the school (.) and then I remember as I was being taken to my classroom I remember I just burst into tears (.) I was just going mad because (.) like (.) I think something silly like (.) my name wasn't on my normal peg (.) where I put my coat so then I was just like (1) like in hysteric tears was just really like (1) annoyed at everything (1) so yes (1) I had all the teachers trying to calm me down like they do in primary school calm me down be nice (.) I just wasn't having it (.) I was just really upset | When you are young, you never think you will grow up and everything seems to be perfect and you know no different. However, change when you're young can be quite difficult to comprehend, as I experienced.<br><br>It was in 1995 and the previous year I had been perfectly happy in nursery. So when my mum took me into school, a horrible surprise hit me when she was leading me somewhere other than nursery. I was being taken away from my sand pits, tiny bicycles and toy cars and over to the big, grey and dull prison which was primary school. Once the fact that I was not going to be in nursery anymore set in, I exploded into hysterical tears. I was uncontrollable and kept storming off, with my mum and teachers having to keep dragging me back.<br><br>My mum then calmed me down and told me that everything would be alright and I was all smiles again.<br><br>However, when I realised that my coat peg wouldn't be in the same place, this again set me off into hysterics. I was inconsolable at this point and it took my mum and teachers ages to calm me down. However, I think I just realised that I wouldn't get my own way and when I went into my new classroom, I was again happy and from then on, my primary school days were very happy.<br><br>Looking back on it now, I can understand why I may have been so upset. Unexpected change can shake even adults and for me it took me by complete surprise. My brain just couldn't understand why everyone was making me leave nursery and I was just a very angry 5-year-old. |

**TELLING A STORY**

# A Written Story

## Writing Your Own Story

Sevim and Tim told anecdotes and then wrote them up as stories. You are going to write up your anecdote (see page 32). (If you prefer to tell a new one to a partner, you could do that instead.)

■ First, think about all the things you can do to make a written story enjoyable and well-structured. Here are some of them:

- giving your story a good title to catch the reader's interest
- introducing the story in a dramatic way
- creating suspense
- using metaphors and similes
- using humour
- including bits of dialogue
- varying sentence lengths to create impact
- summing it all up at the end.

■ Spend a bit of time thinking about how you want to structure your story and what style you want to write it in. For instance:

- Will you start at the beginning of what happened, or at the end?
- Will you use suspense?
- Will you make it frightening, or use humour to bring out the comedy?
- Will you tell it in the present tense, or the past?

■ Write a first draft of your story, then swap with your partner to see if he/she has any good suggestions for making it an even better telling of what happened.

■ Re-write the story, drawing on your partner's ideas.

■ Finally read aloud some of the stories, so that the whole class can hear the written stories.

## Summing Up What You Have Learned

■ Go round the class with each person, in turn, saying something either about the differences between speech or writing, or what makes a good spoken story or a good written story. Your contributions should start with these kinds of openers:

Spoken stories tend to...

Written stories are usually...

A good spoken story often...

A good written story often...

One difference between speech and writing is...

**FROM TALK TO TEXT**

# Keeping in Touch

## Texts, Emails, Blogs & Letters

# Teachers' Notes

Please note: there is no DVD component to this unit.

## A First Look at the Texts

Text 1: Email

Text 2: Blog published on Guardian Online

Text 3: Letter

Text 4: Postcard

Text 5: Entry on Lonely Planet's online message board

Text 6: Personal blog

Text 7: Text message

## Additional Resources

Worksheets, colour images, further resources in PDF format included on the DVD are signalled with this icon:

KEEPING IN TOUCH

# Keeping in Touch

**In this unit you will:**
- explore the different ways people can keep in touch
- look closely at the language used in these different forms of communication
- learn about the different features of spoken and written texts
- think about the advantages and disadvantages of each form.

## A First Look at the Texts

Included on pages 52-54 is a collection of seven texts written by people who are away from home on holiday or travelling for other reasons.

■ Together, read the whole selection of texts and decide which form best describes each text.

| letter | blog | postcard | email | text message |

| online message board |

## Comparing Two Texts

■ Working in pairs, look more closely at *two* of the texts that are very different from each other. Talk about each of these aspects of writing in your two texts.

- Punctuation
- Spelling
- Use of upper and lower case
- Abbreviations
- Use of a formal/informal tone
- Layout
- Use of graphics as well as, or instead of, words

■ What do you think are the points for and against keeping in touch using the different types of text (for example, emails are a very quick way of getting in touch with people but they are less likely to be kept to look back on)? Draw up a 'For and Against' chart like the one shown here to record your ideas.

| Text | For | Against |
|---|---|---|
| Email | 1. Quick way of getting in touch | 1. Not always kept as a record |
|  |  |  |

© English and Media Centre, 2008

LANGUAGE WORKS

# Texts, Emails, Blogs & Letters

## Communication at the Beginning of the 21st Century

Some language experts have described the kind of language used in emails, chatrooms and texting as a blend of spoken and written communication.

- Look at the features of speech and writing listed in the chart below.

- Using the charts on pages 50-51, tick the features of spoken and written communication that apply to each text type.

- Choose one or two things which you find interesting about the way in which the different text types use the features of spoken and written communication. Share these as a class.

- In pairs, look again at *one* of the 'Keeping in Touch' texts on page 52-54. Your teacher will tell you which text to work on. Annotate your text to show the ways in which it uses features typical of spoken communication, written communication or both.

- Feed back your discoveries in class discussion.

| Spoken Communication | Written Communication |
| --- | --- |
| It's often spontaneous and unplanned | There's time to plan what you say |
| It's quick to do | It often goes through a drafting process |
| It's easy to suggest tone by voice, facial gestures etc. | Tone can be suggested by choice of words or symbols |
| A record isn't usually kept of it | It is recorded in print |
| It can go off in all kinds of different directions | It is often carefully structured |
| There's no time lag between replies | There's a time lag between replies |
| It's often informal | It's often quite formal and follows rules of layout |
| It's not a big effort – everyone can do it | It can feel like hard work |
| You can check what someone means | You can't check immediately what someone means |
| It doesn't usually exist beyond the person speaking it | It can continue to exist a long way from the writer (in time and space) |
| More than two people can be involved at once | There usually aren't multiple writers |

LANGUAGE WORKS © English and Media Centre, 2008

KEEPING IN TOUCH

## A Continuum Line

■ On a continuum line like the one shown here, write 'Spoken' at one end and 'Written' at the other.

SPOKEN ←――――――――――――――――――――――――――→ WRITTEN

| letter | blog | postcard |
| email | online message board | text message |

■ In pairs, decide where you would place each of the text types used by the writers in this unit. Be ready to back up your decisions in class feedback.

■ Feed back your decisions using a 'live' continuum line across the classroom. Your teacher will ask different pupils to represent one of the text types and to place themselves on the continuum line. Listen to the reasons for the position each pupil chooses and discuss whether or not they need to move closer to written communication or closer to spoken communication.

■ Identify the text types which most combine the features of both written and spoken communication. Talk about why this might be.

■ What could you call this new type of text which draws on the conventions and features of both spoken and written communication? Spriting? Wriking?

# Simulation

## A Guide to Keeping in Touch

Your school is putting together a guide for parents and students to tell them about the Year 7 residential school trips. One of the sections will include:

– advice for parents about the different ways they can keep in touch during the trip, with the advantages and disadvantages of each

– advice for pupils about the different ways they can keep in touch during the trip, with the advantages and disadvantages of each.

■ You have been asked to write a draft of this section. You will need to bear in mind:

– school trips are often in remote areas and mobile phone reception can be unreliable

– it is school policy to allow students to use their mobile phones for texting only

– pupils will have free access to the internet for 10 minutes each day

– each pupil will receive a free first class stamp.

## Texts, Emails, Blogs & Letters

| Features of Spoken Communication | Letter | Postcard | Email | Blog | Text | Message Board |
|---|---|---|---|---|---|---|
| It's often spontaneous and unplanned | | | | | | |
| It's quick to do | | | | | | |
| It's easy to suggest tone by voice, facial gestures etc. | | | | | | |
| A record isn't usually kept of it | | | | | | |
| It can go off in all kinds of different directions | | | | | | |
| There's no time lag between replies | | | | | | |
| It's often informal | | | | | | |
| It's not a big effort – everyone can do it | | | | | | |
| You can check what someone means | | | | | | |
| It doesn't usually exist beyond the person speaking it | | | | | | |
| More than two people can be involved at once | | | | | | |

## Keeping in Touch

| Features of Written Communication | Letter | Postcard | Email | Blog | Text | Message Board |
|---|---|---|---|---|---|---|
| There's time to plan what you say | | | | | | |
| It often goes through a drafting process | | | | | | |
| Tone can be suggested by choice of words or symbols | | | | | | |
| It is recorded in print | | | | | | |
| It is often carefully structured | | | | | | |
| There's a time lag between replies | | | | | | |
| It's often quite formal and follows rules of layout | | | | | | |
| It can feel like hard work | | | | | | |
| You can't check immediately what someone means | | | | | | |
| It can continue to exist a long way from the writer (in time and space) | | | | | | |
| There usually aren't multiple writers | | | | | | |

© English and Media Centre, 2008

LANGUAGE WORKS

# Texts, Emails, Blogs & Letters

## TEXT 1

**Sally went to Peru to work in a children's centre in her gap year.**

```
From: Sally
Sent: 19 September 2005 01:31
To:
Subject: Cajamarca Update

Hey!
Sorry i've been out of contact for a while, we've been
crazy-busy with running the centre and going on excursions
etc. The project's going really well. Kids are unbelievably
cute, have taken vast numbers of photos of them! Have also
fallen in love with an old, bashed up, open-top truck
which we've been driving around the area in. Last night we
camped in the most amazing place ever, about 2 hours from
cajamarca, in secluded woodland, next to a natural hot
spring, under a full moon, surrounded by fireflies, near
an abandoned house. Weirdly spooky but a very cool place.
We slept in the back of the truck and got up at 5am to swim
in a thermal bath overlooking mountains and forests. Have
been purchasing industrial quantities of cardigans (they're
about 2pounds each and are hand knitted according to our
specifications). Am no longer scared of the ghosts!.
Hope you're all well, keep the news coming from home.
Loads of love,
Sal xxxxxxxxxxxxxxxxxxxxxxxx

p.s. can you forward this to granny r?
```

## TEXT 2

**Rob Bell, project manager at the Energy Saving Trust, travelled to Svalbard in Norway to find out what its glaciers can tell us about climate change. This week he finds himself on polar bear watch.**

It's 4am, I've had three hours' sleep, it's minus 19 outside – and I've just been woken up for an hour's polar bear watch over our camp. How did I find myself in this position?

On the second night of our trek into Svalbard's Arctic wilderness, we set off from the relative civilisation of Longyearbyen on skis, carrying everything we'd need for our three-day camping trip. It took us six hours to cover the 20km or so across the ice fields to the mountains where our next task was finding a suitable spot to set up camp at the foot of the glacier. We would have to build our own snowholes – no Eurocamp facilities out here.

First you dig the entrance to the tunnel, then comes the challenge of sculpting out sleeping chambers. It took two of us a good seven hours to dig the cave which was to be our home for the next three nights. Now I'm quite a fan of DIY, but building my own house is definitely a first and I was rather proud of the results.

Not only did our snowhole give us shelter, it also provided an endless supply of drinking water by melting the snow on our

## Keeping in Touch

stoves. It's quite an experience living so close to the elements – we were in negative temperatures continuously for three days and – despite the sun – the air temperature never rose above about minus 5. It's tough, and not just on the body, as the cold can affect your mood as well.

So that's how I found myself, alone at 4am in 24-hour Arctic daylight, on polar bear watch over my sleeping companions, armed only with my trusty distress pistol and the knowledge that the chance of seeing a polar bear in a region of limited sea ice was extremely small. Hardly an incentive to stay awake, but I'm glad I did. My shift must have coincided with the Arctic rush-hour; I saw Reindeer plodding past, Ptarmigan swooping overhead and an Arctic fox darting across the fresh white surface.

It's moments like this that really bring home the necessity of protecting this unspoilt environment. And for us that means making changes back home in the comfort of our everyday lives.

**TEXT 3**

Dear Mim and Did

It unfortunately pissed with rain this morning. Great start!

No really it's good. The site is a bit annoying as the Tracker's site is way up above the rest of camp so to get down to meals with have to clamber down a verticle mud slope and often falling on your arse.

The other people are a mixed bunch. One the one hand you've got the younger lot, a bit like last time. their ok but a bit boring. On the other hand you've got the hard you're lot, smoking about 40 fags a day (don't stress I'm not going to start) Everyone seems nice. There's another girl from school in our group too! Alison unfortunately not my faveourite person! But she's quiet so it doesn't matter.

We had a group camp fire last night.

I hope you're having a great time wherever you are but the time you get this you'll soon be coming home. I'm sure you'll see some fasinating ….urm things. The food's ok, but we haven't had many meals yet.

I had a brilliant time with Doreen. Guys & Dolls was wicked!

I've got to go play killer frisby now.

Love, me

# TEXTS, EMAILS, BLOGS & LETTERS

## TEXT 4

Here we are having a beer beside the harbour in kassiopi. It is beautiful! It's lovely and warm even when the sun is in (v. rarely!) and there is a lovely soft breeze so it isn't oppressive! We are going on some lovely boat trips as we have decided the sea is the only way to travel. See you soon. l.o.l e + c

## TEXT 5

Cycling around Central Park Posted by noddyjoe 2 May 2007
What better way to see the weird and wonderful sights of Central Park on a beautiful sunny day? We had planned to go rollerblading but didn't have the gear or the skill. We hired 'cruiser' bikes from the boathouse for $9 per hr and proceeded to cruise around the car free one way road that takes you on a tour around the whole park. It was just glorious. Not too energetic or time consuming. It took about 40 minutes at a gentle pace. It was on a sunny Saturday so we got to see every sort of New Yorker and tourist doing what they wanted to do - playing baseball, 'football', chilling out, frisbee, juggling, dancing, shouting, singing, getting married, sailing, people watching and on and on. It was the highlight of our trip.

## TEXT 6

Hiiiiiii everyone! Seems we've barely had time to scratch ourselves or sleep - let alone hop on the internet!! So New York.....WOWWWWW. Some random thoughts:

- The taxis relly are yellow
- The school busses really are yellow too
- The stature of liberty isnt as big as you would expect
- There's cute little squirrel things running around Battery Park
- The loss of the twin towers is afr more devestating than just the lives lost, its is such a massive emptiness in the sky line where they onece stood
- Times Square freaking rocks
- It really is the city that never sleeps
- There are street vendors everywhere selling drinks, hot dogs, pretzels and nuts
- The city is soooooo easy to find your
- way around (or if you are dean SOOO hard) but seriously, the streets/avenues are all numbered and it's so logical
- You CAN get sunburnt when it's only 16 degrees and overcast (Dean is lobster red on his forehead the poor fella!)
- Now....as for what we have actually done....

## TEXT 7

```
Hi - we are having great time! Frosty night -v cold n caravan
glad not in tent sunny now tho, sea beautiful- not swimming
today - too freezing :(. A cooked lovely meal - fresh fish.
Hom today. Hope all gd with you. x x x SENDER: SNORK
```

# Texts for Tots
## The Language of Picture Books

# Teachers' Notes

To teach this unit you will need:

- a class set of 8-10 copies of *Where the Wild Things Are*
- *John Brown, Rose and the Midnight Cat*. As this picture book is now out of print, a slide show and reading of the text is included on the DVD. Secondhand copies are widely available from online booksellers such as Amazon Marketplace.

You could substitute these texts with others and adapt the activities.

For the extension activity, it would be helpful to have copies of other tales by Beatrix Potter.

## DVD Menu

The following activities have a DVD element signalled with this icon:

| Selectable section | Duration | Onscreen title | See page |
|---|---|---|---|
| Babies with books | 2 mins 30 | | 65 |
| Learning to read *(Reading strategies)* | 5 mins | | 67 |

## Additional Resources

Worksheets, colour images, further resources in PDF format included on the DVD are signalled with this icon:

TEXTS FOR TOTS

# Texts for Tots

**In this unit you will:**
- explore the language of picture books
- look at the relationship between words and pictures
- use what you have learned to write your own picture book
- think about how children learn to read.

## Where the Wild Things Are

### Reading the Words

■ On page 58 are the words of a children's picture book, without the pictures. Read the words, then look at these statements and decide whether you agree or disagree with each one. You might decide that you agree with part of the statement but not all of it. Look closely at the story to find evidence for your views.

| | Statement | Agree/Disagree | Evidence |
|---|---|---|---|
| 1. | There is lots of repetition. | | |
| 2. | All the words are simple ones. | | |
| 3. | The sentences are very long, which is surprising in a picture book. | | |
| 4. | It sounds like poetry. | | |
| 5. | All the sentences are short to help a child follow the story. | | |
| 6. | The language is a bit old-fashioned. | | |
| 7. | The story uses rhyming words. | | |
| 8. | Some bits of the story are hard to follow because there are gaps where things are left unsaid. | | |
| 9. | There are too many 'ands' in the story. | | |
| 10. | It's good to have direct speech - the things that people actually say. | | |
| 11. | The use of rhyme makes some phrases memorable. | | |
| 12. | The language is too difficult for small children. | | |

© English and Media Centre, 2008

# THE LANGUAGE OF PICTURE BOOKS

> The night Max wore his wolf suit and made mischief of one kind and another his mother called him 'WILD THING!' and Max said 'I'LL EAT YOU UP!' so he was sent to bed without eating anything. That very night in Max's room a forest grew and grew – and grew until his ceiling hung with vines and the walls became the world all around and an ocean tumbled by with a private boat for Max and he sailed off through night and day and in and out of weeks and almost over a year to where the wild things are. And when he came to the place where the wild things are they roared their terrible roars and gnashed their terrible teeth and rolled their terrible eyes and showed their terrible claws till Max said 'Be still!' and tamed them with the magic trick of staring into all their yellow eyes without blinking once and they were frightened and called him the most wild thing of all and made him king of all the wild things. 'And now,' cried Max, 'let the wild rumpus start!' 'Now stop!' Max said and sent the wild things off to bed without their supper. And Max the king of all the wild things was lonely and wanted to be where someone loved him best of all. Then all around from far away across the world he smelled good things to eat so he gave up being king of where the wild things are. But the wild things cried, 'Oh please don't go – we'll eat you up – we love you so!' And Max said, 'No!' The wild things roared their terrible roars and gnashed their terrible teeth and rolled their terrible eyes and showed their terrible claws but Max stepped into his private boat and waved good-bye and sailed back over a year and in and out of weeks and through a day and into the night of his very own room where he found his supper waiting for him.

## Reading the Whole Story

In this activity, you are going to explore how, in picture books, words and pictures work together to make meaning.

- Read *Where the Wild Things Are* out loud, looking at the pictures.

- Talk about your first responses. Did you like the story? Did the pictures make a difference?

### Tracking Words and Images

- Go through the book from the first page to the last, tracking the balance of words and pictures, using the chart on page 61 to record your findings. The example below shows you what to do.

|  | **Words** | **Pictures** |
| --- | --- | --- |
| Page 1 | 1 line | None |
| Page 2 | None | Medium size in centre of page |

- What do you notice about the changes in the use of pictures as the book progresses? Why do you think this happens?

## Texts for Tots

### Looking More Closely

The first double page spread from *Where the Wild Things are* is re-printed on page 60.

- Look carefully at the two pages and, as a class, share anything you notice about the words, the picture and the way they work together.

Now read what one person noticed about this first page, in the box at the bottom of this page.

- Share out the pages or double-page spreads for each group to present to the rest of the class, explaining your ideas about the way the words and pictures work.

- Present your pages to the whole class.

- Now talk about which of the following statements you agree with, and add any others of your own:

**1** The story is a simple one.

**2** There are lots of different meanings in the story and the more you read it the more you see.

**3** The pictures carry some of the meanings in the story.

**4** Pictures are a sort of language that you have to read like words.

**5** Simple is best when it comes to children's picture books.

**6** It's good to have lots of layers of meaning, so you see more and more, the more you read.

#### Looking More Closely – An Example

There's just one line of print, showing Max in his wolf suit. The words just say he's making mischief but the picture shows exactly what *kind* of mischief it is. He's got a great big hammer (dangerous for a small boy) and is banging nails into the wall. He seems to have taken his sheet off his bed and his poor cuddly toy looks a bit miserable, being hung up from a coat hanger. Max's mouth is downturned and serious, as if he's determined to be naughty. His wolf suit makes him half child, half animal – it's a sleepsuit with a make-believe element but Max is being quite 'wild' in his behaviour too. He's standing on books – maybe it shows that, for Max, books are for standing on, not for reading! The one line of the story isn't finished, so it urges you to turn over the page to find out more.

# The Language of Picture Books

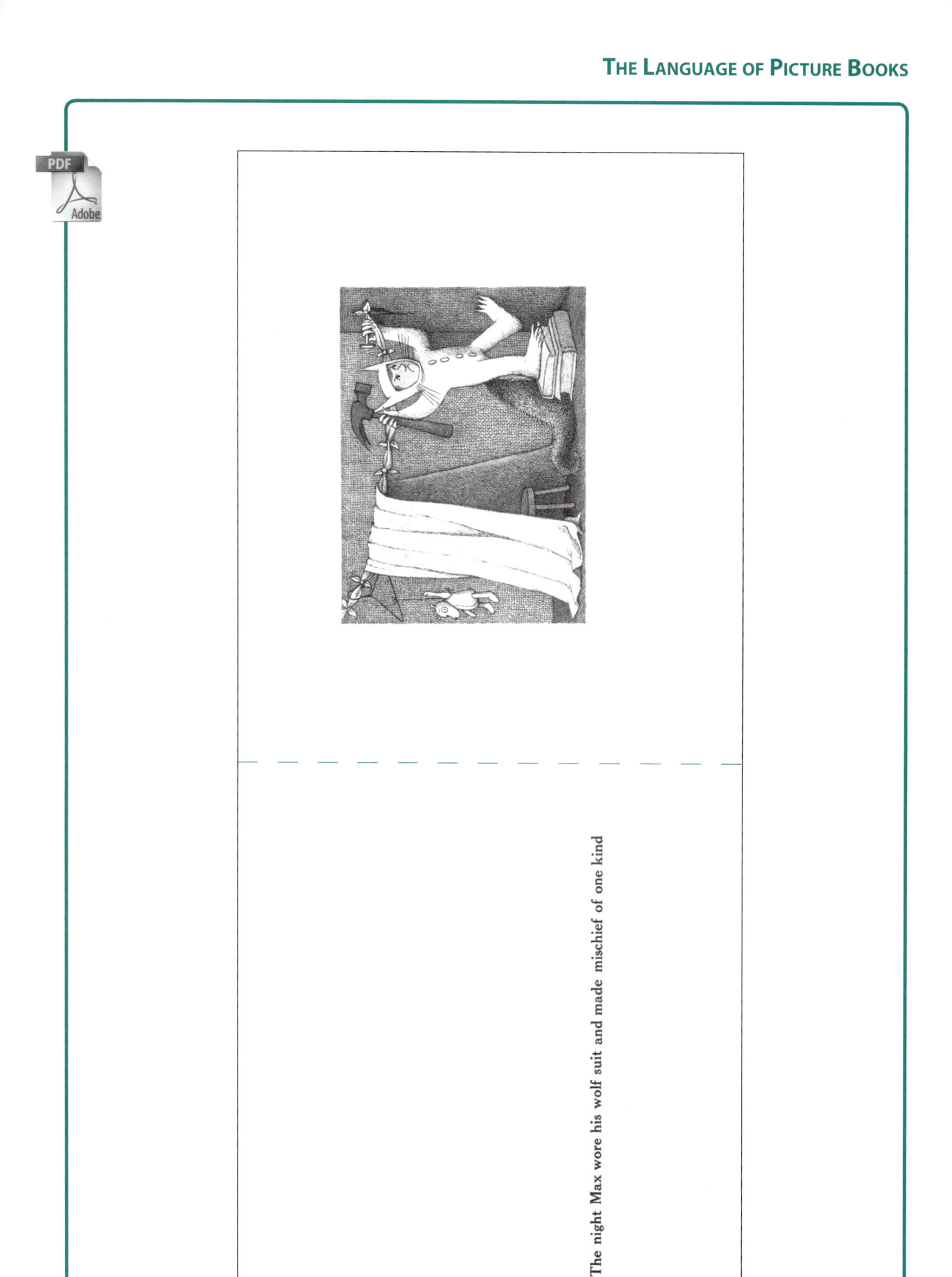

The night Max wore his wolf suit and made mischief of one kind

## TEXTS FOR TOTS

### Tracking Words and Images

| Spread | Words | Pictures | Comment |
|---|---|---|---|
| 1 | | | |
| 2 | | | |
| 3 | | | |
| 4 | | | |
| 5 | | | |
| 16 | | | |
| 7 | | | |
| 8 | | | |
| 9 | | | |
| 10 | | | |
| 11 | | | |
| 12 | | | |
| 13 | | | |
| 14 | | | |
| 15 | | | |
| 16 | | | |
| 17 | | | |
| 18 | | | |
| 19 | | | |

THE LANGUAGE OF PICTURE BOOKS

# John Brown, Rose and the Midnight Cat

To pause the reading, press 'Pause' on your remote control, or the space bar on your computer.

## A Close Look at Sentences

- Listen to the story being read aloud to you, looking at the pictures on the slideshow, up to 'and when supper time came, he was still thinking'.

- Talk about what you think of the story so far, how much you think it would appeal to small children and why.

- The words from the beginning of the story are included in the chart below, without the pictures.

- What do you notice about the kinds of sentences the writer has used? For each sentence, decide whether it is **simple**, **compound** or **complex**. The explanation of different types of sentences on page 63 will help you.

- Talk about the effect of the choice of sentence types, remembering that this is a book to be read by small children.

| Sentence | Simple | Compound | Complex | Compound-complex |
|---|---|---|---|---|
| 1. Rose's husband died a long time ago. | | | | |
| 2. Now she lived with her dog. | | | | |
| 3. His name was John Brown. | | | | |
| 4. John Brown loved Rose, and he looked after her in every way he could. | | | | |
| 5. In summer he sat under the pear tree with her. | | | | |
| 6. In winter he watched as she dozed by the fire. | | | | |
| 7. All year round he kept her company. | | | | |
| 8. 'We are all right, John Brown,' said Rose. | | | | |
| 9. 'Just the two of us, you and me.' | | | | |
| 10. One night Rose looked out of the window and saw something move in the garden. | | | | |
| 11. 'What's that in the garden, John Brown?' she said. | | | | |
| 12. John Brown would not look. | | | | |

**TEXTS FOR TOTS**

## Sentence Types

**Simple, compound and complex sentences**

**Sentences are made up of clauses**, or parts of the sentence. For instance there are three clauses in this sentence:

> The boy earned some extra pocket money/
>
> by washing the car/
>
> and used it to go to the pictures.

A **simple sentence** has only one clause, for instance:

> The boy earned some extra pocket money.

A **compound sentence** links two or more clauses, using connectives like 'and', 'or' or 'but', for instance:

> The boy earned some extra pocket money and used it to go to the pictures.

A **complex sentence** links two or more clauses, using words like 'by', 'because', 'when' and 'although'. The clause connected by one of these words can't stand on its own and make sense, for instance:

> The boy earned some extra pocket money by washing the car.

Here 'by washing the car' makes no sense on its own.

If a sentence has both, like the first one you looked at, it is called a **compound-complex sentence.**

© English and Media Centre, 2008    LANGUAGE WORKS

# THE LANGUAGE OF PICTURE BOOKS

## Writing the End of the Story

- There are five more pages till the end of the story. Try writing your own version of the end of the story, using the same sentence structures and style as the writer.

- Share your endings and give each other help in changing the language, to make it fit the style of the original.

- Now read the original ending, watching the slideshow on the DVD. Talk about how it compared with your own, and how successful you found it as an ending to the story.

## Summing up What You Have Learned

- If you have read both *Where the Wild Things Are* and *John Brown, Rose and the Midnight Cat*, look at these statements and decide which you agree with:

| 1 | Children's books always use simple words. |
|---|---|
| 2 | Children's books always have short, simple sentences or compound sentences. |
| 3 | Children's books use pictures and words to create meanings together. |
| 4 | Pictures are as important as words in children's books. |
| 5 | Repeated patterns are important to help children remember a story. |
| 6 | The language of a picture book should have enough in it to make you want to read over and over again. |

- As a class, create a list of statements that you can all agree on, summarising what you think about the language of children's books. Feel free to add your own ideas to the ones you have chosen from above.

## Reading Other Picture Books

- Look through a few other picture books. (You could bring in a favourite one from when you were small or borrow one from the library.) Choose one to focus on closely.

- Think about the use of words and pictures in your book. Draw on what you learned earlier in this unit to write a paragraph or two about what you notice.

- Present your book and your ideas to the whole class.

**TEXTS FOR TOTS**

*19 mins*

# Learning to Read

## Babies with Books

Research has shown that long before they go to school, children learn the building blocks of reading by listening to books being read to them, turning the pages, looking at pictures, lifting flaps and so on. Here are some of the 'pre-reading' skills identified by researchers as being particularly important.

1. **Handling books**, for instance turning pages.
2. **Looking at and recognizing pictures**, for instance by gazing or laughing at a favourite picture, or pointing at pictures.
3. **Understanding events or pictures in a book**, for instance imitating an action in a book or talking about what happens in it.
4. **Engaging in story-reading behaviour**, such as babbling in imitation of a story, or pretend-reading.

■ Look at the three video clips of very small children with books.

Gemma is 9 months old    Mathilda is 15 months    Ellie is 24 months

Which of the four pre-reading skills do you see each of these children demonstrating? Record your observations in the chart below, using the following key:

Not at all ✘

Beginning to do this ✓

Some of the time ✓✓

A lot of the time/confidently ✓✓✓

|  | Gemma | Mathilda | Ellie |
|---|---|---|---|
| Handling books, for instance turning pages. | | | |
| Looking at and recognizing pictures, for instance by gazing or laughing at a favourite picture, or pointing at pictures. | | | |
| Understanding events or pictures in a book, for instance imitating an action in a book or talking about what happens in it. | | | |
| Engaging in story-reading behaviour, such as babbling in imitation of a story, or pretend-reading. | | | |

© English and Media Centre, 2008

# THE LANGUAGE OF PICTURE BOOKS

## Your Own Memories

■ What are your own first memories of being read to by adults, or learning to read? Talk in small groups, using these questions to help jog your memory.

   a. What were your favourite books?

   b. Do you remember being read to at infant school or primary school? Where did it happen? Sitting on the carpet? In assembly? What was it like?

   c. When/how did you learn your alphabet and the sounds letters make? Did you take reading books home in a folder?

   d. Were you told stories? By whom (teachers, parents, grandparents)? What kind (fairytales, folktales, other stories)?

   e. Did you learn to read in more than one language? Were you read to in different languages?

## Your Ideas About Reading

■ What does it mean to be able to read? Look through the statements listed here and share your ideas about reading:

| 1 | Reading is when you can spell out the words and pronounce them properly. |
|---|---|
| 2 | You have to understand all the words before you can say you can read. |
| 3 | Reading is when you can read out loud without stumbling. |
| 4 | Adding expression to your voice shows you can really read. |
| 5 | You don't have to understand all the words to be able to read and enjoy a story. |
| 6 | Confident readers read in their head, not out loud. |
| 7 | Even the best readers do not understand all the words in all the stories they read. |

**TEXTS FOR TOTS**

## Reading Strategies

You are going to watch Wise, Michael, Josh and Alex reading to their teacher. Wise, Michael and Josh are reading *John Brown, Rose and the Midnight Cat*. Alex is reading *Where the Wild Things Are*.

■ Watch the clip through once, making a note of anything that strikes you about the boys' reading, for example:
- how interested or involved each boy is in the story
- the strategies each boy uses when he is stuck
- the role the teacher plays.

**Wise**

**Josh**

The chart below lists some of the strategies beginning readers use to help them.

■ Watch the DVD clip again, this time focusing more closely on the strategies the boys use to help them read and understand the story. How do the strategies that the boys use compare with those you use when reading?

■ Share your observations as a class. Which strategies do you think are most helpful?

■ Together draft a 5-point plan for parents to help them support their children when learning to read.

**Alex**

**Michael**

| Strategy | Wise | Josh | Alex | Michael |
|---|---|---|---|---|
| Sounding out individual words | | | | |
| Looking at the pictures | | | | |
| Talking about the pictures | | | | |
| Using a finger to follow the words | | | | |
| Using the sentence punctuation | | | | |
| Guessing the meaning from the rest of the sentence | | | | |
| Questioning from the teacher | | | | |
| Asking the teacher for help | | | | |
| Waiting for the teacher to tell them the answer | | | | |

© English and Media Centre, 2008     LANGUAGE WORKS

# Creative Writing

## Writing a Picture Book of Your Own

**Planning Your Story**

■ Use everything you have learned about the language of picture books, to produce one of your own. If you can, you could produce it as a text with pictures, perhaps working in Art lessons as well as English lessons, or using I.T. to make it look professional. If you want a few ideas to get you started you could use *one* of the following prompts.

1. Use one of these title suggestions:
   - Mrs Pumpkin
   - A Day Out
   - The Magic Football
   - Squeaky, the School Mouse
   - Where's Claire?
   - The Elephant and the Snake

2. Use the first line of one of these published picture books as your first line:
   - Lucy was afraid of nearly everything.
   - Princess Smartypants did not want to get married.
   - We're going on a bear hunt.
   - Brown Bear, Brown Bear, what do you see?
   - 'Hello Dad,' said Bernard.

3. Tell your own picture book version of a famous fairytale or fable such as:
   - Hansel and Gretel
   - Aesop's fable of the hare and the tortoise
   - Rama's quest to rescue the princess Sita
   - The Three Little Pigs
   - An Anansi story

■ Use the planning checklist on page 69 to help you keep in mind the kind of language you want to use. Tick the ones you want to feature in your story and keep going back to your list to keep track of whether you're managing to include them.

# Texts for Tots

## Instructions to an Artist

- Write a set of instructions to an artist, explaining the kind of pictures you would want to illustrate your story.

## An Audience for Your Story

- If you can, try out your story on a few children, to see how well it works. This might be a younger brother or sister, a child you babysit for, or your teacher might be able to organise a visit to a local infant school.

## A Planning Checklist

| My story will try to: | |
|---|---|
| use repetitions of words and phrases | |
| use mainly simple and compound sentences | |
| use a combination of words and pictures | |
| use some of the techniques of poetry, such as rhyme | |
| play with words, for instance using nonsense words or made-up words | |
| have page breaks to encourage children to want to turn over the page | |
| use simple words | |
| use a mixture of simple words and more unfamiliar words | |
| use Standard English | |
| use other dialects of English | |

# Extension Activity

## The Language of *Peter Rabbit*

The original story of *Peter Rabbit* was written by Beatrix Potter in 1902. A new version, adapted by David Hately, was produced by Ladybird Books and first published in 1997, almost 100 years later.

In this activity, you will be comparing the two versions.

- Look at the two front covers below and on page 71. What differences do you notice? Talk about why you think there are these differences and what expectations they give you about the books themselves.

**Version 1 (1902)**

**TEXTS FOR TOTS**

**Version 2 (1997)**

*[Cover image: Ladybird edition of "The tale of Peter Rabbit" – Based on the original story by Beatrix Potter]*

- Look at an extract of the words only from each version (on page 72). Decide which is from 1902 and which from 1997. What helped you reach your decision?

- Look more closely at the texts:
    - Which words has Hately decided to change and what difference does this make?
    - Has Hately changed the sentence structures in any way? Longer or shorter sentences? Simpler or more complex?
    - Which uses more direct speech and why?
    - Has Hately changed any of the details of the story? If so, why do you think this might be?

- Talk about which version you think small children today would like better and why.

## Writing Your Own Adaptation

- Choose another tale by Beatrix Potter. Write an adaptation of an extract from the tale, making your own decisions about how much you want to change to appeal to a modern child. Write a paragraph to go with it, explaining your decisions.

© English and Media Centre, 2008

# THE LANGUAGE OF PICTURE BOOKS

## Version 1

| Page | Text | Comment |
|---|---|---|
| 1 | Once upon a time there were four little Rabbits and their names were – Flopsy, Mopsy, Cotton-tail, and Peter.<br><br>They lived with their Mother in a sand-bank, underneath the root of a very big fir-tree. | |
| 2 | 'Now, my dears,' said old Mrs. Rabbit one morning, 'you may go into the fields or down the lane, but don't go into Mr. McGregor's garden: your Father had an accident there; he was put in a pie by Mrs. McGregor.' | |
| 3 | 'Now run along, and don't get into mischief. I am going out.' | |
| 4 | Then old Mrs. Rabbit took a basket and her umbrella, and went through the wood to the baker's. She bought a loaf of brown bread and five currant buns. | |

## Version 2

| Page | Text | Comment |
|---|---|---|
| 1 | Once upon a time there were four little rabbits. Their names were Flopsy, Mopsy, Cotton-tail and Peter. They lived in a burrow at the root of a big tree. | |
| 2 | One day they were allowed to play outside. 'Stay near home,' said their mother. 'Please don't go to Mr McGregor's garden.'<br><br>'Why not?' asked Peter.<br><br>'Because he doesn't like rabbits,' answered Mrs. Rabbit. 'He will try to catch you.' | |
| 3 | Mrs. Rabbit made sure that Flopsy, Mopsy, Cotton-tail and Peter were wearing their warm clothes.<br><br>She waved them goodbye as they went out to play. Then she put on her bonnet and shawl and set off to the baker's. She wanted to buy a loaf of bread and some buns. | |

# Mathilda Speaking: Learning to Talk

# Teachers' Notes

## DVD Menu

DVD clips are signalled with the following icon: **DVD**

| Selectable section | Duration | Onscreen title | See page |
|---|---|---|---|
| In the high chair – 12 months | 45 secs | | 80 |
| Reading with Mum – 15 months | 1 min | | |
| Scarf and beads – 20 months | 1 min 10 | | |
| Sticklebrick car – 24 months | 1 min 10 | | |
| Let's pretend – 24 months | 1 min 10 | | |
| Turning off the light – 25 months | 40 secs | | |
| Taking to herself – 28 months | 40 secs | | |
| Talking with friends – 2 years, 7 months | 2 mins 30 secs | | |

## Additional Resources

Worksheets, colour images, further resources in PDF format included on the DVD are signalled with this icon:

## Teachers' Notes

### Language Points to Draw Out in Each Clip

You might want to select the most interesting points from these descriptions of Mathilda's development rather than analysing everything in detail.

| | | |
|---|---|---|
| 1: In the high chair (12 months) | Responds to speech with gestures, facial expressions and a catch-all word 'iss'. Mathilda listens to what Bonny and Dan say, 'answers' their questions and laughs when they do. | 'iss' |
| 2: Reading with Mum (15 months) | Mathilda is reading one of her favourite books with Bonny. She exhibits 'reading' behaviour, turning the pages, and engaging with the pictures by pointing to the animals and opening the flaps. Answers Bonny's questions with the appropriate animal noise. Towards the end of the clip Mathilda shows she is beginning to initiate conversation, naming the bird 'tweet' without being prompted. | Animal noises ('moo', 'iaow', 'tweet') <br><br> 'yesss' |
| 3: Scarf and beads (20 months) | Mathilda has just come back from the childminder. She has dressed herself in Bonny's scarf and is having fun taking it on and off and announcing when she is doing this. Her vocabulary has noticeably increased. She confidently repeats words. After Bonny asks 'Shall I help you', Mathilda adopts the phrase 'help you' to mean 'can you help me?'. She hasn't yet mastered the difference between using 'me' and 'you' (personal pronouns). She also seems to identify 'help you' as one word so probably couldn't be said to be using more than single words. She later asks for help in the same way without being prompted. She initiates a conversation about the beads on Bonny's necklace, pointing to the small beads, calling them 'baby'. With Bonny she names the colours of the beads. | on; off; help you <br><br> baby bead <br><br> yellow; red <br><br> orange |
| 4: Stickle-brick car (24 months) | This is an interesting clip for several reasons: Mathilda is confidently initiating conversations and using language to make things happen. This is shown clearly in her insistence that the car has 'orange wheels' even when Bonny misunderstands what she is saying. She is no longer simply repeating words and phrases but answering questions independently. Her use of the possessive 'lady's' shows a marked development in her grammatical understanding. She is definitely using two-word strings here. | car; lady's <br><br> orange wheels <br><br> yeah; man <br><br> seat; whoopsie |

# Teachers' Notes

| | | |
|---|---|---|
| 5: Let's pretend (24 months) | Mathilda is using language to play: she understands the increasing tension of the countdown and takes a full role in the make-believe game. She uses imperatives, uses two words together and is beginning to construct word strings. She refers to herself as 'Tilda' rather than 'I' and Bonny as 'mummy' rather than 'you', even when addressing her directly, so hasn't yet fully grasped the use of personal pronouns. | sleep there; mummy<br><br>Tilda sleep sofa<br><br>feet ('weet')<br><br>night night<br><br>mummy up |
| 6: Turning off the light (25 months) | This extract reveals a considerable development in Mathilda's language acquisition: she takes the lead in asking a question and answers Bonny's query with a full sentence and with emphatic. She uses intonation appropriately and now refers to herself as 'I'. | light off<br><br>yes I can reach it |
| 7: Talking to herself (28 months) | In this extract Mathilda is shown talking to herself as she plays, using 'this' and 'that' to distinguish between the toy cars. This is egocentric language – talking aloud to yourself as a running commentary is typical of early language development. She uses possession confidently 'Jon's'. She also seems to be taking pleasure in her ability to use language, repeating the words with different intonations and singing. She also makes a joke based on the connection between her own name (Mathilda Kate Oliver Johns) and those of her Aunt and Uncle (Kate Oliver and Jon). | this one Kate's/Jon's<br><br>Kate's house<br><br>that one<br><br>Kate Oliver John's house |
| 8: Talking with friends (2 years 7 months)<br><br>Jess is 3 years 9 months | Although Mathilda and her cousin, Jess, are confident speakers (each taking the lead, using language to express feelings, make demands, get things done), their lack of conversational etiquette is clear: They do not always engage with other or take turns, often carrying on parallel conversations. They do not always follow politeness principles! | we here daddy<br>we wait and Jon come<br>That be big lorry<br>Coming<br>That way<br>I being careful with ironing board<br>All flat<br>I ironed that for her<br>This not done<br>I find it for you<br>I help<br>There you go Jess |

LANGUAGE WORKS © English and Media Centre, 2008

## Teachers' Notes

### Language Development Milestones

This brief outline may help you work with your students on Mathilda's language development.

| From: | Babies and children begin to… |
| --- | --- |
| Birth: | hear and respond to sounds |
| 1 month | smile spontaneously and in response to someone |
| 1-2½ month | recognise their parents |
| 2-4 months | coo making sounds like ah or eh (vowel sounds) |
| 3-6 months | imitate speech sounds |
| 4-8 months | laugh out loud; babble individual or monosyllabic sounds like ba or ga (vowels and consonants) |
| 5-9 months | babble repeated sounds like bababab, lalalala, etc (vowels and consonants) |
| 6 months | respond appropriately to friendly and angry tones; use intonation in the sounds they make |
| 6-9 months: | follow a one-step command with a gesture (e.g. will respond appropriately if someone asks for an object with hand held out) |
| 6-10 months | understand individual words (mummy, daddy, no) |
| 7-11 months | follow a one-step command without a gesture |
| 7-12 months | use dada and mama to mean dad and mum |
| 9-14 months | say their first word other than dada or mama |
| 10-15 months | point to objects that they want |
| 11-20 months | use 4-6 words other than mama/dada, family names or names of pets; practice inflection; show awareness that speech has a social value |
| 14-20 months | understand a 'two-step' command such as 'Find your shoes and bring them here.' when given without a gesture |
| 16-20 months | communicate what they want using single words such as 'juice', 'more' etc; may overextend for instance by using 'dog' to refer to all animals or 'daddy' to refer to all men. |
| 18 months | use about 5-20 words, mainly nouns; understand about 50 words; repeat words or phrases over and over |
| 16-24 months | use an increasing number of words, experiencing a vocabulary 'spurt' from 50 words to approximately 150-300 words |
| 18-22 months | put together simple two-word sentences. These are usually either two content words to show location, possession or action. They may also use also noun-verb combinations like 'Daddy go' |
| 19-26 months | use pronouns ('me', 'you' etc) although these may be used incorrectly (for example me and I are often confused) |
| 24 months | have speech which is over 50% intelligible by strangers; begin to use 'my' and 'mine' |
| 24+ months | put together sentences with several content words, often strung together without any sense of grammatical order. |

© English and Media Centre, 2008

# Teachers' Notes

| | |
|---|---|
| 24-36 months | master the morphology of language and start adding affixes like 'ing'; use function words like 'the' and 'is' and put together grammatically correct sentences |
| 26-32 months | hold conversations with 2-3 simple sentences put together |
| 27-30 months | understand two prepositional commands ('put the cup on top of the table' or 'next to the book') |
| 30 months | use pronouns correctly |
| 3 years | have speech 75-90% understandable by strangers; have a vocabulary of 900-1000 words; use some plurals and past tenses, although may overgeneralise for instance, using the -ed suffix to indicate past tense for verbs like 'go' and 'think', as in 'go-ed' and 'think-ed'; handle three word sentences easily |
| 3-4 years | name 4 colours |
| 4 years | have speech which is fully understandable by strangers; speak aloud as they carry out activities |
| 5 years | use descriptive words (both adjectives and adverbs); use fairly long sentences including some compound and some complex sentences; have speech which is generally grammatically correct |
| 6 years | have speech which is completely understandable; can tell a story about a picture, seeing relationships between objects and happenings |
| 8 years | relate involved accounts of events, including those which have happened in the past; use complex and compound sentences with ease; use grammatically correct speech with greater ease; can carry on conversation at rather adult level; follow fairly complex directions with little repetition |

**Sources consulted**

http://www.childdevelopmentinfo.com/development/language_development.shtml

http://www.asha.org/public/speech/development/01.htm

http://www.asha.org/public/speech/development/default.htm

http://www.medem.com/search/article_display.cfm?path=n:&mstr=/ZZZWKQVIQDC.html&soc=AAP&srch_typ=NAV_SERCH

http://www.nidcd.nih.gov/health/voice/speechandlanguage.asp#mychild

http://www.ldonline.org/article/6313

http://www.blankees.com/baby/speech/

http://pediatrics.about.com/cs/growthdevelopment/l/bl_lang_milesto.htm

http://www.med.umich.edu/1libr/yourchild/devmile.htm

MATHILDA SPEAKING

# Mathilda Speaking

**In this unit you will:**
- think about your own memories of learning to speak
- watch a series of video clips of one baby beginning to use language
- explore some of the stages children go through as they learn to speak.

## Learning to Talk

What do you know about the way you learned to talk? What about younger brothers, sisters or other babies you know?

■ In small groups or as a class, share what you already know about the way babies and young children learn to speak.

Included in the boxes below are some of the things you might remember about learning to talk.

■ Add any other memories you have. You could also ask people who knew you when you were little. Choose one topic to talk about in small groups.

| Nursery rhymes | Listening to stories | Talking to friends | 1st words |

| What you called other people | Quiet or noisy? | Your name for a favourite teddy or toy | A 'secret' language |

| Your first joke | Words you used wrongly | Talking to imaginary friends | What you were called |

| Songs with actions | Family words | Looking at books | Words you pronounced wrongly |

© English and Media Centre, 2008                                LANGUAGE WORKS

LEARNING TO TALK

# Watching Mathilda

You are going to watch video clips recorded over 18 months showing Mathilda with her mum, dad and friends. You will see her using gestures and sounds, then one or two words till by the time she is 2½ she is stringing together short sentences and speaking with confidence. In the DVD clips you will see, or hear, about the following people:

Mathilda

Bonny: Mathilda's mum

Dan: Mathilda's dad, who is doing the filming

Kate: Mathilda's aunt

Jon: Kate's husband

Jess: Mathilda's cousin who is 3¾

## A First Viewing

The chart below describes the different situations you are going to see Mathilda and Bonny in, along with some of the key words and phrases Mathilda is using.

■ Use the chart to help you follow what is happening in each clip. You could use the 4th column to make a note of anything that interests you about Mathilda's language.

| Clip | What's Happening? | Mathilda's Key Words | Your Notes |
| --- | --- | --- | --- |
| 1: In the high chair (12 months) | Mathilda is in her high chair at breakfast talking to her mum (Bonny). | 'iss' | |
| 2: Reading with Mum (15 months) | Mathilda is reading one of her favourite books with Bonny. | Animal noises ('moo', 'iaow', 'tweet'); 'yesss' | |
| 3: Scarf and beads (20 months) | Mathilda has just come back from the childminder. She has dressed herself in Bonny's scarf and is having fun putting it on and taking it off. | on; off; help you; baby bead; yellow; red; orange | |

80  LANGUAGE WORKS © English and Media Centre, 2008

# Mathilda Speaking

| | | | |
|---|---|---|---|
| 4: Stickle brick car (24 months) | Bonny and Mathilda decide to play with sticklebricks. Mathilda suggests they should build a car. | orange wheels; car; lady's; yeah; man seat; whoopsie; | |
| 5: Let's pretend (24 months) | Mathilda organises Bonny into playing a game of pretend sleeping, telling her mum what to do. | sleep there; mummy; Tilda sleep sofa; feet ('weet'); night night; mummy up | |
| 6: Turning off the light (25 months) | Mathilda wants to play at turning the light on and off. | light off yes I can reach it | |
| 7: Talking to herself (28 months) | Mathilda is at the kitchen table playing while Bonny is doing the washing up behind her. She is talking and singing to herself as she plays. | this one Kate's/Jon's Kate's house that one Kate Oliver John's house | |
| 8: Talking with friends (2 years 7 months) | In this short montage of clips Mathilda is shown playing with, and talking to her cousin. | we here daddy That be big lorry I being careful with ironing board All flat I find it for you There you go Jess | |

The chart on page 82 lists some of the stages babies and children go through as they learn to talk.

- As you watch the DVD clips for a second time, record the stage you think Mathilda is at by ticking the relevant box. Use the following system to show whether she is just beginning to use this feature, is using it more securely, or is using it with some confidence.

✓ – just beginning

✓✓ – uses it more securely

✓✓✓ – uses it with confidence

- Share your decisions as a class.

**LEARNING TO TALK**

## Tracking Mathilda's Language Development

| | Listening | Babbling | Gestures/ Pointing | Making Sounds | Single Words | Repeating Single Word | Two Words | Word Strings | Taking the Lead |
|---|---|---|---|---|---|---|---|---|---|
| 1: In the high chair (12 months) | | | | | | | | | |
| 2: Reading with Mum (15 months) | | | | | | | | | |
| 3: Scarf and beads (20 months) | | | | | | | | | |
| 4: Sticklebrick car (24 months) | | | | | | | | | |
| 5: Let's pretend (24 months) | | | | | | | | | |
| 6: Turning off the light (25 months) | | | | | | | | | |
| 7: Talking to herself (28 months) | | | | | | | | | |
| 8: Talking with friends (2 years 7 months) | | | | | | | | | |

MATHILDA SPEAKING

## Charting Mathilda's Progress

- After watching all the DVD clips, look again at the first one, filmed when Mathilda was just 12 months. In your own words, describe the progress she has made in her ability to communicate and use language in just 18 months.

- Use your chart, the lists of key words and the notes you made during your first viewing to talk about your impressions of the way Mathilda is learning how to communicate and use language.

- In pairs, use your findings to create a graph of Mathilda's language development over the 18 months shown in the DVD clips, using the example below as a model.

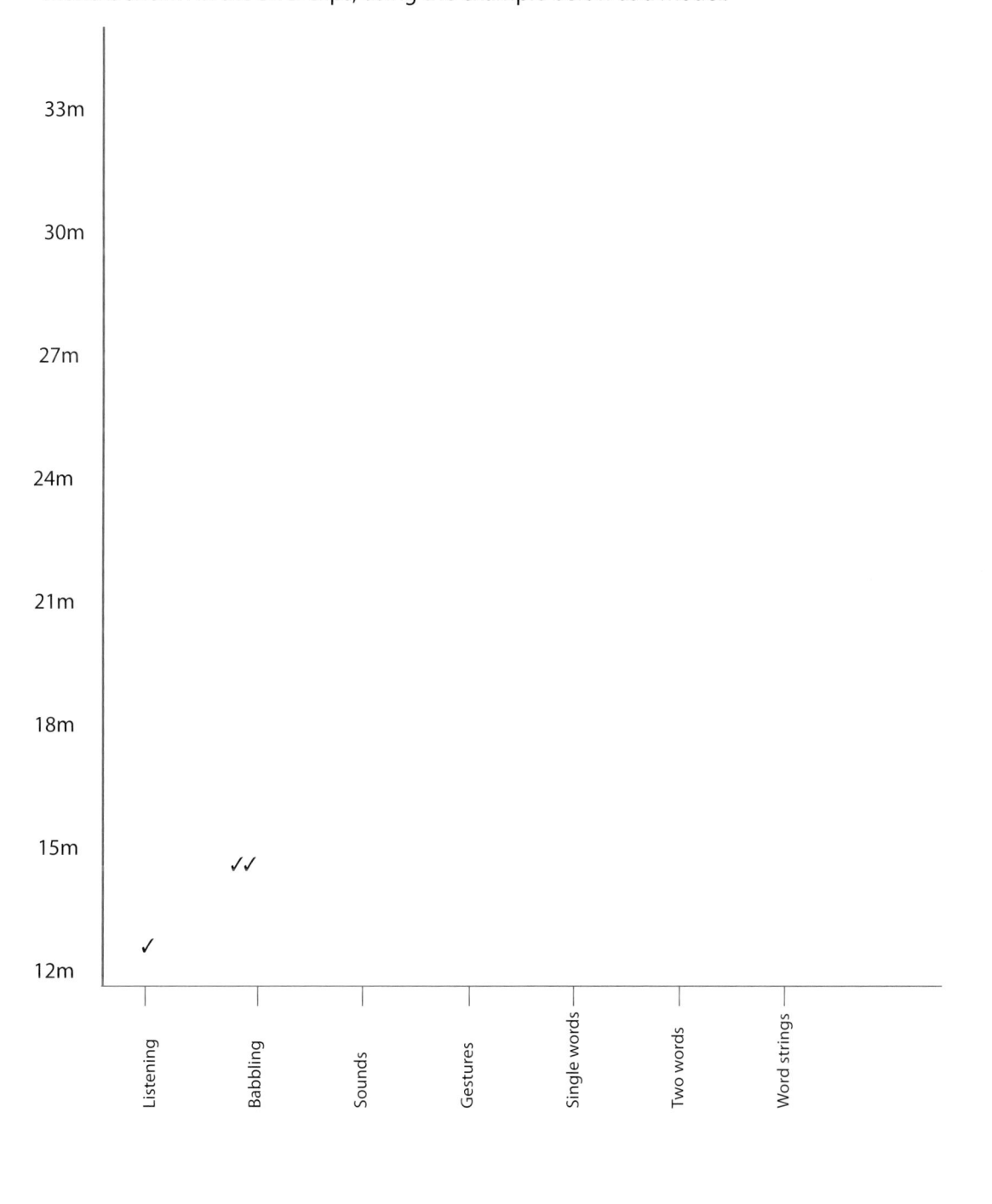

| | Listening | Babbling | Sounds | Gestures | Single words | Two words | Word strings |
|---|---|---|---|---|---|---|---|
| 33m | | | | | | | |
| 30m | | | | | | | |
| 27m | | | | | | | |
| 24m | | | | | | | |
| 21m | | | | | | | |
| 18m | | | | | | | |
| 15m | | ✓✓ | | | | | |
| 12m | ✓ | | | | | | |

© English and Media Centre, 2008     LANGUAGE WORKS

# Learning To Talk

# Developing Children's Language

## What Bonny Does

- As a class, share your ideas about the ways in which parents and carers can help children develop their ability to communicate with gestures, sounds and speech.

- Watch the DVD clips again, this time paying particular attention to the way in which Bonny (her mum) plays and talks with Mathilda.

- In pairs, pick out three things Bonny does that you think will help Mathilda with her language development.

- As a class, take it in turns to feedback what you noticed about the strategies Bonny uses to help Mathilda.

- Use the chart below to collect together the strategies you think are most helpful and your reasons for thinking this.

|  | Bonny's Strategy | Reason Why |
|---|---|---|
| 1: In the high chair (12 months) | | |
| 2: Reading with Mum (15 months) | | |
| 3: Scarf and beads (20 months) | | |
| 5: Sticklebrick car (24 months) | | |
| 6: Let's pretend (24 months) | | |
| 7: Turning off the light (25 months) | | |
| 8: Talking to herself (28 months) | | |
| 9: Talking with friends (2 years 7 months) | | |

MATHILDA SPEAKING

## Helping Your Child to Speak – a Guide for Parents

■ You are going to write a short guide for parents called 'Helping Your Child to Speak'. To do this you should use what you have learned about:

- the way you learned to speak
- your own observations of babies and children learning to speak
- what you have learned from watching Mathilda and Bonny
- the stages children go through when learning to speak
- what older children and adults can do to help children.

In your guide you could include:

- a chart showing the stages children go through when learning to speak
- a tiny bit of transcript (taken from the DVD of Mathilda and Bonny or from children you know) with your comments on what is happening
- top tips on how to help a child learning to speak
- amusing things children say.

© English and Media Centre, 2008 LANGUAGE WORKS

**Learning To Talk**

# Playing with Words
## Games to Explore Language

# Teachers' Notes

Some of these games need advance preparation or resources, for instance 'One Hundred Words' needs to be photocopied (and ideally laminated) in advance.

Instructions to teachers appear on the pages marked **T** and are tinted pale green.

Worksheets for students are on pages marked **S**

Not all the games have student sheets.

## Additional Resources

Worksheets, colour images, further resources in PDF format included on the DVD are signalled with this icon:

PLAYING WITH WORDS

# One Hundred Words – 3 Variations

> **The cards:**
> - can be used for exploratory activities and games
>
> **The activities:**
> - encourage students to come to some understandings of key concepts of language by investigating words for themselves
> - might last just fifteen or twenty minutes, or might expand to take more time, depending on how far you want to take them.
>
> What follows are three different ways of using the word cards, with some teachers' notes to support their use.

## 1. One Hundred words – A Sorting Game

■ Photocopy the words (on pages 93-94), cut them up and put them in envelopes. You could use different colours for each set of cards, so that it's easy to reassemble them if they get muddled together. If possible laminate the sheets before cutting them up so they have a longer shelf life.

■ Organise the class into small groups, with a table or tables to work on.

■ Give each group an envelope with the 100 words in it.

■ Ask them to choose words that seem to them to 'go together' for whatever reason and put them into little clusters.

■ Pause the game. Ask groups to think about how they've clustered the words. At this stage you might just collect their ideas about how they've categorised words. You might want to help them to clarify how they've categorised them (see some of the suggestions on page 90).

■ Ask them to continue the game by finding *other* ways of grouping the words.

■ Pause the game again to collect ideas about the categories and hear what words they've put into their categories.

■ Either at the end of the game (or during the game if pupils need some extra support) you might help students to label their categories and add in ones they might not have come up with.

© English and Media Centre, 2008

Possible ways of categorising the words:

- by meaning (all words to do with a particular topic)
- by word class (for example all verbs, all nouns, all adverbs)
- by origin (words that have come into the language from other languages)
- by levels of formality or informality
- by whether they're spoken or written
- by shape, appearance or length (for example polysyllabic, monosyllabic)
- by context or register (legal language, academic language)
- by time (words that are no longer used, words that are bang up to date)
- by sound or register (words that rhyme, words that use onomatopoeia, words that sound good)
- homonyms for example 'tear' (words that look the same but sound different and have two different meanings)
- words that express a sound or exclamation
- words that can be put together to make a sentence
- words that can be put together to make a story

■ Together, you might sum up what's been learned, for example:

- different ways in which one might think about language, for example where words come from (**etymology**), what role words play in a sentence (**syntax**), what words mean (**semantics**), what words are used in informal or formal contexts (**discourse/ register**), how words differ in terms of length and structure and so on.
- anything that has been learned about the words themselves (for example that academic words tend to be longer than slang words or that some words are both nouns and adjectives).

## Another Variation on the Game

You could decide on just one category for sorting in advance – possibly doing it as a 10-minute activity and repeating it on another occasion with different categories. This would allow you to define the particular aspect you want students to learn (for example to focus on the origins of words, or to focus on word classes). The advantage of this is that you could use it to teach a particular concept. The downside is that it makes it less exploratory and investigative.

PLAYING WITH WORDS

### 2. One Hundred Words – Lucky Dip

This could be done as a whole class, or in small groups.

- Put the cards into a hat or container. Ask a student (or one student from each group) to pick a word.

- Give a time limit for students to brainstorm their word from as many different angles as they like. Once they're finished you can add in more ideas to take them further and extend their knowledge about language.

Example: YES

- the opposite of no
- but it can mean no, or I'm not sure, if the tone of voice is changed
- or it can be used as a question for example 'Yes?' as in 'What do you want?'
- people use it more than no because they don't like saying no, for example 'Yes but'
- it's the object of a joke in *Little Britain* – 'yes but, no but' – which shows how it can mean nothing at all
- it has lots of colloquial versions and sound versions – 'yep', 'yeah', 'mmm'
- it can be replaced with a nod of the head
- it can be a sentence in its own right, even though it doesn't have a verb (This is called a 'minor sentence'.)
- sometimes it gets missed out but is understood as being there, for example 'Do you want a present?' '[yes] Please!'

© English and Media Centre, 2008

LANGUAGE WORKS

GAMES TO EXPLORE LANGUAGE

**T**

## 3. One Hundred Words – Thinking About Sentences and the Roles Words Play in Sentences

■ Use the words to write sentences, finding words that are interchangeable and thinking about what role they perform in a sentence. (It could be used to explore simple, compound and complex sentences.) This might be best done on an interactive whiteboard, as a shared activity, before letting students try it on their own.

- Ask students to select words to write a simple sentence.
- Now ask them to make the sentence longer by adding words.
- Do the same again and possibly a third time.
- Look at whether they can substitute words, for example substituting adjectives, nouns and so on. Explore the way in which some words could be placed in more than one position i.e. words that can be both a noun and a verb, for example 'book' as in 'a book' or 'book' as in 'Book me a ticket.'

Here are two examples of how it might work:

**Adding words**

| The | | bloke | | | | wishes | to | dance. | | |
|---|---|---|---|---|---|---|---|---|---|---|
| The | dazed | bloke | | | | wishes | to | dance. | | |
| The | dazed | bloke | | | | wishes | to | dance | like | me. |
| The | dazed | bloke | who | is | cool | wishes | to | dance | like | me. |

**Substituting words**

| The | young | bloke | wishes | to | dance. |
|---|---|---|---|---|---|
| The | comical | bloke | wishes | to | dance. |
| The | comical | cow | wishes | to | dance. |
| The | comical | cow | wishes | to | fly. |

## Playing with Words

| | | | | |
|---|---|---|---|---|
| because | might | may | gosh | a |
| go-cart | Marcus | Crunchie | catches | read |
| danced | was | the | fly | as |
| dread | like | she | me | vex |
| dislike | at | biro | unsure | theirs |
| oink | imagine | where | boo | psychological |
| win | victory | sleepily | rockstar | funny |
| comical | cow | go | ouch | vodka |
| bungalow | cool | oy | reggae | wicked |
| its | I | restaurant | sassy | to |

## Games to Explore Language

| | | | | |
|---|---|---|---|---|
| yes | no | book | table | ran |
| skipped | fell | flew | is | feels |
| thinks | believed | healthy | actually | really |
| OK | grey | his | hers | isn't |
| magnificent | can't | on | supermarket | jumps |
| wow | why | what | knew | fiendishly |
| slowly | knew | he | it | dog |
| crazily | web | dastardly | metatarsal | in |
| and | sherbert | quadruped | tear | madam |
| sure | you | shop | wishes | can |

PLAYING WITH WORDS

# Squabble

**Using the pieces from a Scrabble set, this game:**
- reinforces work on spelling, especially patterns such as prefixes, suffixes, verb endings and so on.
- teaches about word classes or other aspects of word level grammar.

## 1. Basic Squabble

**Before starting the game**

- Play the game in groups of three or four.

- Turn all the Scrabble pieces face down in the middle of the table.

**The game**

- Take turns to turn over a letter. As each letter is revealed, the players should see if they can call out a word of four letters or more that is made by using any of the up-turned letters.

- When a word is called out, that player takes the letters and puts them in front of them. The word now 'belongs' to them. That person re-starts the game by turning over the next letter in the middle.

- As more letters are revealed, anyone who can see a way of adding to that word, or changing it, or making an anagram of it, can call the new word out and take it themselves. To grab someone else's word you have to use every letter in their word – you can't leave any behind! But you can add as many as you like from the revealed letters on the table. You can't make a new word by adding an 's' to form a plural.

**The end of the game**

- The game ends when all the letters have been revealed and no-one can grab any more words from each other. The winner is the person who has the most letters in front of them.

**An example of how it works**

- Player 1 calls out 'heat' and takes the word.
- An 'h' is revealed in the middle of the table, Player 2 notices it and calls out 'heath', taking the word from Player 1.
- An 'l' is later revealed and Player 1 notices it and calls out 'health', taking the word back.
- A 'y' is later revealed. Player 3 calls out 'healthy', taking the word from Player 1.
- No-one else manages to alter the word, so Player 3 gets 7 points at the end, 1 point for each letter of 'healthy'.

## 2. More Advanced Variations

- You can set restrictions on the type or length of word players have to make, for example only nouns or words with two or more syllables or words of five or more letters.

© English and Media Centre, 2008

LANGUAGE WORKS

GAMES TO EXPLORE LANGUAGE

# Word Class Rush

> **This game:**
> - teaches about word classes through an active approach.
> - helps students to go beyond very simple definitions since some words fit more than one word class, depending on their function in a sentence.

## Version 1

- Arrange furniture so it's easy for students to move around.

- Make nine cards with different word classes on them: Noun, Determiner, Verb, Adjective, Adverb, Pronoun, Preposition, Conjunction, Interjection. Stick them up on the classroom walls, at well-spaced intervals.

- Have a list of words available (for example: I, skip, happily, over, delicious, sausages, but, Oh!, to, his )

- Shout them out and the whole class (or half the class, with one half just watching from the middle) has to surge towards the word class they think is the right one.

## Version 2

- Use some of the words on the 'Hundred Words' cards blown up and handed out, so that each student has one card.

- Students have to go to the correct word class with their card.

- Talk as a whole group about any words which could go in more than one word class. Allow the pupils with this card to choose which word class to go into.

- Once pupils are organised into word class groups, play a game of creating random sentences, almost like consequences. For instance:
  - The teacher says, 'Let's start our sentence with a determiner' and any student from the determiner group is chosen.
  - The teacher asks what's needed next and it should emerge that an adjective or a noun is needed.
  - The group decides which and a random person is chosen. The teacher asks which word class could/should come next and so on.

PLAYING WITH WORDS

T

# Lingo

> **This game:**
> - gives pupils familiarity with terms for word classes and a chance to apply their knowledge
> - teaches that words are used in different ways and that the choice of word class sometimes varies according to context (for example if students can explain their use of 'break' as a noun – as in lunch break – that's fine)
> - teaches students to think more flexibly about language and grammar.

## Version 1

To play this game, students will need a photocopied Lingo card (see the example on page 98). To play Version 1, you will have to make several different cards so that each student pair has a different set of words.

■ Pupils are each given a card with 36 words on each.

■ The teacher selects 'calls' at random:

- Eyes down – Find a NOUN
- Sixty six – Find a PREFIX
- Get your kicks – Cross off a SUFFIX
- Walk on the kerb – Find yourself a VERB
- Find a word that's superb – Where's the ADVERB?
- Your brain is like a sieve – Find an ADJECTIVE
- Go to town – Find a PRONOUN
- Look down – Find a POSSESSIVE PRONOUN
- This is your mission – Find a PREPOSITION
- Be selective – Find a CONNECTIVE
- A tiny little particle – Find a(n) (IN)DEFINITE ARTICLE

■ Pupils write the word class under their word

## An Alternative Lingo

■ Play the game using cards with word classes printed on them, rather than words and call or show individual words/parts of words (car, walked, an, –ly etc.) that students categorise and cross off, writing the word underneath. When someone calls out 'Lingo', having completed their card, the teacher will need to check that a word class has been identified correctly.

The Alternative Lingo cards can be used for all students over and over again, calling out different words.

© English and Media Centre, 2008     LANGUAGE WORKS    **97**

GAMES TO EXPLORE LANGUAGE

**Lingo Sample**

| | An | Happy | Under | Run | Car | Merrily |
|---|---|---|---|---|---|---|
| Word Class? | | | | | | |
| | Whale | Because | She | He | Under | Frog |
| Word Class? | | | | | | |
| | Their | Go | The | Purchase | With | -ly |
| Word Class? | | | | | | |
| | Soon | With | Expensive | Sunflower | His | In |
| Word Class? | | | | | | |
| | Often | Sofa | Dictionary | Anti- | -tion | Who |
| Word Class? | | | | | | |
| | If | A | Her | Cabbage | Soccer | Paint |
| Word Class? | | | | | | |

**Version 2 Lingo Card**

| CARD 1 | Preposition | Adjective | Pronoun | Verb | Noun | Adverb |
|---|---|---|---|---|---|---|
| Word? | | | | | | |
| CARD 2 | Noun | Suffix | Pronoun | Prefix | Adjective | Verb |
| Word? | | | | | | |
| CARD 3 | Possessive Pronoun | Verb | Definite Article | Possessive Pronoun | Indefinite Article | Preposition |
| Word? | | | | | | |
| CARD 4 | Verb | Connective | Adverb | Noun | Pronoun | Adjective |
| Word? | | | | | | |
| CARD 5 | Adverb | Suffix | Noun | Preposition | Prefix | Pronoun |
| Word? | | | | | | |
| CARD 6 | Adjective | Preposition | Connective | Adverb | Verb | Noun |
| Word? | | | | | | |

LANGUAGE WORKS © English and Media Centre, 2008

PLAYING WITH WORDS

# Puns, Playing with Words and Misunderstandings

**These activities:**
- provide a fun context for investigating language features.

The cards below describe some of the language features used in jokes.

■ As a class, read the six descriptions of the ways you can use language to make jokes. Check that everyone understands the language feature described.

■ In pairs or small groups, pupils read the jokes and talk about which language feature each joke is playing on and place it on the correct pile (see cards on page 100).

■ Pupils tell each other favourite jokes and identify the language feature each one relies on.

■ Individually or in pairs, pupils use what they've learned to experiment with making up their own jokes.

---

1. **Homophones** – words that sound the same but have a different spelling and meaning.

   e.g. 'flu' and 'flew', 'weak' and 'week', 'maid' and 'made'

2. **Homonyms** – words which are spelled the same but have different meanings.

   e.g. 'pitch' ('tar' and 'throw'), 'lead' ('metal' and 'guide'), 'left' (opposite of 'right' and 'abandoned')

3. **Mime words and phrases** – words and phrases that sound similar.

   e.g. 'What do hedgehogs eat for breakfast?' 'Prickled onions'.

4. **Malapropisms** – words used incorrectly.

   e.g. 'Listen to the blabbing [babbling] brook'

5. **Spoonerisms** – changing round the letters of words.

   e.g. 'par cark' for 'car park'

6. **Deliberately misunderstanding the grammar or the rules of conversation.**

   e.g. 'Where did King John sign the Magna Carta?' 'At the bottom.'

   'A Scotsman takes all his money out of the bank once a year for a holiday; once it's had a holiday he puts it back again.'

   'How do you make a cat drink? Put it in a liquidizer.'

© English and Media Centre, 2008     LANGUAGE WORKS

GAMES TO EXPLORE LANGUAGE

| HOMOPHONES | HOMONYMS |
| --- | --- |
| MIME WORDS | MALAPROPISMS |
| SPOONERISMS | MISUNDERSTANDING GRAMMAR |

**PLAYING WITH WORDS**

S

| What's Dracula's favourite pudding? | What do you call a boy with a seagull on his head? | Why do cows have bells? |
|---|---|---|
| I scream. | Cliff. | Because their horns don't work. |

| Why don't witches wear a flat hat? | How do you make an apple puff? | What sort of lights did Noah's ark have? |
|---|---|---|
| Because there's no point to it. | Chase it round the garden. | Floodlights. |

| What jumps from cake to cake and tastes of almonds? | What do you give a sick pig? | Why are vampires so stupid? |
|---|---|---|
| Tarzipan. | Oinkment. | Because they're suckers. |

Knock, knock.
Who's there?
Joanna.
Joanna who?
Joanna big kiss?

My dog has no nose.
How does he smell?
Terrible.

Where does your sister live?
Alaska.
Don't worry I'll ask her myself.

© English and Media Centre, 2008

LANGUAGE WORKS **101**

# GAMES TO EXPLORE LANGUAGE

**S**

---

**Dad says the monster is just a pigment of my imagination.**

Dad says the monster is a figment of my imagination.

---

**What would you get if a monster trod on Batman and Robin?**

Flatman and Ribbon.

---

**What do you get if you sit under a cow?**

A pat on the head.

---

**What's wrong with a man who has jelly in one ear and sponge cake in the other?**

He's a trifle deaf.

---

**Which snakes are good at maths?**

Adders.

---

**How do you make antifreeze?**

Hide all her jumpers.

---

**Why is it dangerous to play cards in the jungle?**

Because of all of the cheetahs.

---

**Why did the apple turn over?**

Because it saw the swiss roll.

---

**The problem was it was all a complete lack of pies.**

The problem was it was all a complete pack of lies.

---

**What did the big telephone say to the little telephone?**

You're too young to be engaged.

---

**Which vegetable is strong and green?**

A muscle sprout.

---

**Why couldn't the butterfly go to the dance?**

Because it was a moth-ball.

---

102   LANGUAGE WORKS                                                © English and Media Centre, 2008

**The Apprentice**

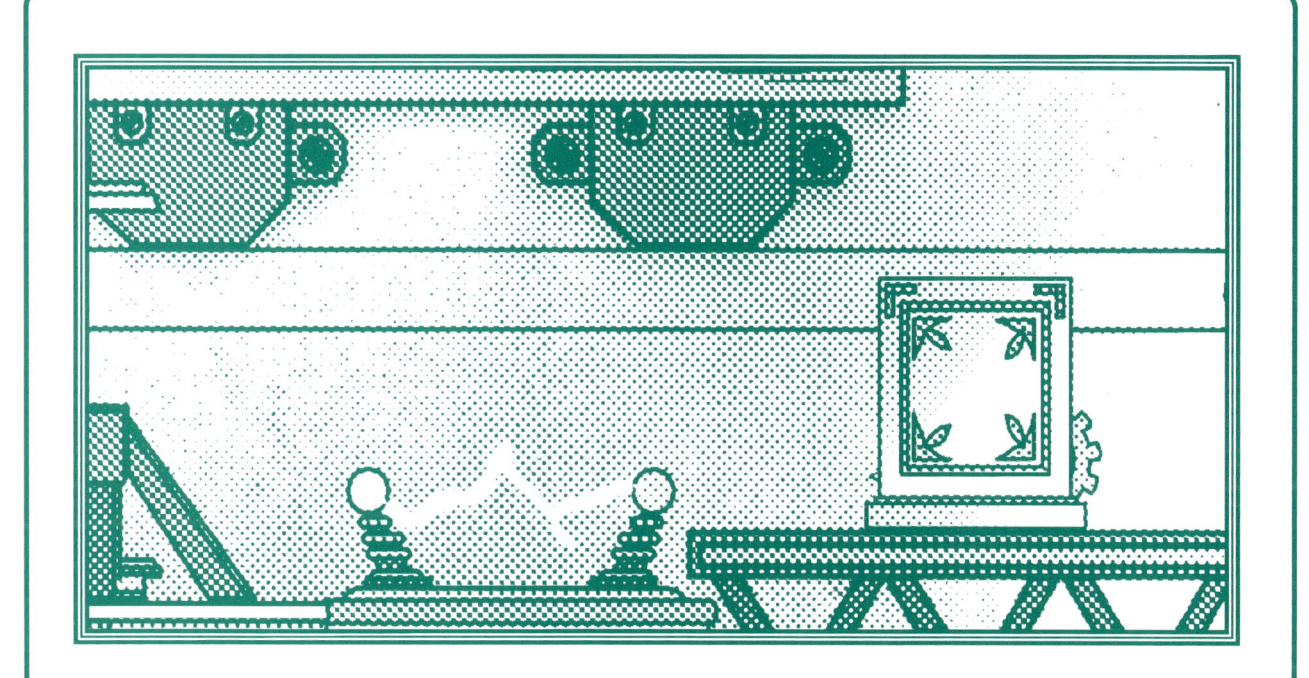

# THE APPRENTICE
## How Groups Talk

# Teachers' Notes

## DVD Menu

The following activities have a DVD element signalled with this icon: **DVD**

|  | Selectable section | Duration | Onscreen title | See page |
|---|---|---|---|---|
| Alan Sugar's apprentices | Deciding the group name | 4 mins |  | 106 |
|  | Planning the calendar | 5 mins |  | 108 |
| Year 9 apprentices | Planning the calendar | 4 mins | Deciding on a name | 122 |
|  |  |  | Deciding on a slogan |  |
|  |  |  | Planning the calendar |  |
|  | Pitching the idea | 5 mins | Planning the pitch | 123 |
|  |  |  | Making the pitch |  |
|  |  |  | Re-making the pitch |  |
|  | Reflections on leadership | 1 min 30 |  | N/A |

## Additional Resources

Worksheets, colour images, further resources in PDF format included on the DVD are signalled with this icon:

# THE APPRENTICE

# Alan Sugar's Apprentices

**In this unit you will:**
- look closely at the way people behave when working in groups, focusing on two short clips from *The Apprentice*
- analyse the apprentices' use of language, body language and tone of voice
- develop strategies for working effectively in groups and think about the way language can be used to help
- take part in a group simulation
- reflect on your own use of language when working in a group.

## Before Watching

In the boxes below are some fragments from the group discussion you are going to watch.

■ Listen to the fragments being read out loud, then discuss what they tell you about the discussion.

- Does it seem to be a constructive discussion?
- Do any of the phrases leap out at you as being particularly helpful or unhelpful, and if so, which ones and why?

■ As a class try organising the phrases into groups. When you are happy with your groups of phrases give each one a title, for example 'Expressing an opinion'.

■ Brainstorm any other words, phrases or sentence starters which you think might be useful in group discussion and add these to the most appropriate group.

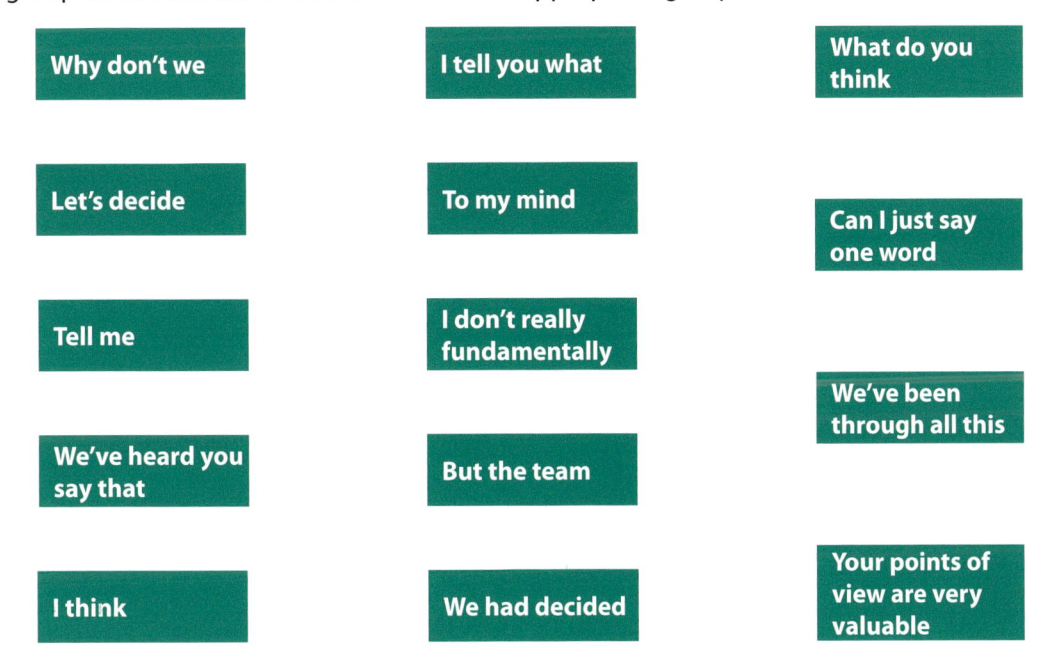

| Why don't we | I tell you what | What do you think |
| Let's decide | To my mind | Can I just say one word |
| Tell me | I don't really fundamentally | We've been through all this |
| We've heard you say that | But the team | |
| I think | We had decided | Your points of view are very valuable |

© English and Media Centre, 2008     LANGUAGE WORKS    **105**

# How Groups Talk

You are now going to watch two short clips from *The Apprentice*. The first extract shows the two groups choosing their name. The second extract shows the two groups working on the task they have been set: to plan, design, produce and market a calendar to be sold in aid of Great Ormond Street Children's Hospital.

## Deciding the Group Name

- Watch the two groups choosing their name. You could annotate the photos below with key words to help you remember the role each contestant plays in the discussions (for example, 'leader', 'lots of ideas').

- In groups share your first responses to the two groups, using the statements on page 107 to get your discussion started.

- As a class feed back the main points of your discussion.

**Nargis**    **Alexa**    **Ruth**    **Jo**

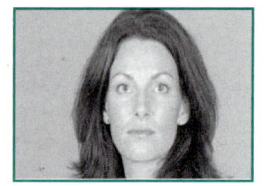

**Karen**    **Sharon**    **Michelle**    **Samuel**

**Syed**    **Ansell**    **Tuan**    **Paul**

**Mani**    **Ben**

# THE APPRENTICE

## Discussing the Groups – Statements

| Statements | Men | Women | Both |
|---|---|---|---|
| The group decided very quickly what they wanted to do and got on with it. | | | |
| The group considered lots of possibilities before deciding what to do. | | | |
| Everyone had chance to put forward their idea. | | | |
| There was a clear leader in this group. | | | |
| The group made sure everyone understood the task. | | | |
| People were more concerned with getting their idea accepted than with getting the task done most effectively. | | | |
| The group planned carefully. | | | |
| Only a few people made the decisions with the others happy to go along with them. | | | |
| This group was equally good at listening as at talking. | | | |
| No-one in this group listened to anyone else. | | | |
| No-one in this group took the lead. | | | |
| There were too many people trying to lead this group. | | | |
| Some of the people in this group were very frustrated by the way a few people dominated. | | | |
| There was no discussion. | | | |
| There was lots of discussion. | | | |
| The group was good at moving the discussion on. | | | |
| Certain people in the group were very skilful at using language to deal with disagreements. | | | |
| Certain people in the group used language in ways which made disagreements worse. | | | |
| The body language in this group suggested everybody was getting along. | | | |
| The body language in this group revealed the tensions even when the words being spoken suggested everybody was getting along well. | | | |

© English and Media Centre, 2008     LANGUAGE WORKS

# How Groups Talk

## Planning the Great Ormond Street Calendar

- Watch Velocity (the women's group) and Invicta (the men's group) planning their calendars in aid of Great Ormond Street Hospital. Use the images below and on page 106 to help you identify the different contestants. You might also find it helpful to follow the discussion on the transcripts on pages 116-120.

### Looking More Closely – Analysing the Discussion

Linguists, psychologists, sociologists, management experts and teachers are just some of the people who are interested in the way people work together in groups, the roles they adopt, the language they use and their body language. These people have developed different ways of talking about and analysing group discussion. These are sometimes called **frameworks** or **models**. Three of these frameworks are included on pages 109, 111 and 113:

- The Roles People Take
- Conversation Analysis
- Non-Verbal Communication (body language and tone of voice)

- Work in groups of between three and five. Each group is going to become an expert in one of these frameworks and use it to analyse the two 'Apprentice' groups as they work together to plan, design and produce the calendar in aid of Great Ormond Street Hospital.

*Note: Ben, who took a lead role in choosing the name of the group, was fired after the first task and so is not part of the Great Ormond Street Hospital calendar discussion.*

# THE APPRENTICE

## Framework 1 – the Roles People Take

People working in groups often take on a particular role in the discussion. This might be because they are generally an enthusiastic person or it may be because they have decided to adopt an enthusiastic role in a particular discussion. Some of the roles people might adopt at different points in a discussion are listed below.

You are going to use this framework to help you analyse the discussions in *The Apprentice*.

- **Conciliator** (someone who smoothes things over between people)
- **Initiator** (the one who gets things going)
- **Facilitator** (the one who helps the group work together)
- **Reflective thinker** (the one who carefully considers the ideas and different ideas)
- **Leader**
- **Ideas generator**
- **Enthusiast**
- **Listener/Observer**
- **Objector** (the person who points out all the possible problems in a plan)
- **Supporter**
- **Bystander** (the person who opts out)
- **Organiser** (the person who keeps everyone on task, for example by reminding the group of the requirements of the task or of the deadline)
- **Summariser** (the person who sum things up)
- **Attacker** (the aggressive person or the one who attacks other people's ideas)
- **Show-Off** (the person who likes to speak whether or not they've got anything constructive to say)

■ In your group, each person should choose one contestant to focus on from the two lists below.

Velocity (the women's group): Nargis, Jo, Ruth, Alexa, Karen

Invicta (the men's group): Samuel, Syed, Ansell, Tuan, Paul

As you watch the discussions, look for the role (or roles) which best fit your contestant. You could note these on the transcripts on pages 116-120.

■ Highlight the words and phrases that seem to be typical of the role or roles your contestant takes in the discussion.

■ Share your thoughts about the roles taken by the contestants during the discussions. Do people seem to adopt one role or do they move between roles? Which roles seem to you to be the most helpful in making the group discussion go well?

■ After you have watched the clips, use the transcript and your annotations to complete the chart on page 110. You might find it helpful to work as a group on this part of the task.

## How Groups Talk

### Framework 1 – Roles People Take

| Name | Roles taken in the discussion | Evidence from the transcript | Behaviour |
|---|---|---|---|
| Nargis | | | |
| Jo | | | |
| Ruth | | | |
| Alexa | | | |
| Karen | | | |
| Samuel | | | |
| Syed | | | |
| Ansell | | | |
| Tuan | | | |
| Paul | | | |

# THE APPRENTICE

## Framework 2 – Conversation Analysis

One way of analysing talk is to focus on the way discussions work. This is often called conversation analysis. It includes looking closely at the following:

- who decides what is spoken about (**sets the agenda**)
- how the group takes turns (**turn-taking**)
- who interrupts and how the rest of the group react to this (**interruptions**)
- how long each person speaks for in one go (**length of utterances**)
- how people in the group show they are working together, for example, by nodding or saying 'You are so right about that.' (**co-operative signals**)
- how the subject is changed and by whom (**topic shifting**)
- who keeps a check on how the group is getting on, for example 'Look, we're spending too long on this section' or 'You're not being helpful' (**self-monitoring**).

You are going to use this framework to help you analyse in more detail the way the discussions in *The Apprentice* work.

■ In your group, each person should choose one contestant to focus on from the two lists below.

Velocity (the women's group): Nargis, Jo, Ruth, Alexa, Karen

Invicta (the men's group): Samuel, Syed, Ansell, Tuan, Paul

■ As you watch the extracts of the two 'Apprentice' groups, annotate the transcripts on pages 116-120 with what you notice about the discussion (for instance, highlight the points at which the subject is changed to show who sets the agenda).

■ After you have watched the clips, use your annotations to complete the chart on page 112. You might find it helpful to work in pairs on this part of the task, then share your notes with the rest of the group.

■ Using the transcripts, choose an example from *The Apprentice* to illustrate each of the features of a discussion.

■ Write two or three sentences describing anything that particularly strikes you about the way the two 'Apprentice' groups discuss their tasks and work together (for example, are there lots of short utterances with interruptions? Is it always the same person who introduces new topics? Does the group work well together to move the discussion on?).

# How Groups Talk

**Framework 2 – Conversation Analysis**

| Feature | The men's group | The women's group |
|---|---|---|
| Agenda-setting | | |
| Turn-taking | | |
| Interruptions | | |
| Length of utterances | | |
| Co-operative signals | | |
| Topic shifting | | |
| Moving the discussion on | | |
| Self-monitoring | | |

THE APPRENTICE

## Framework 3 – Non-Verbal Communication

Research shows that up to 70% of communication is non-verbal. In other words what we say is only a small part of what we communicate to our listener. We 'say' a great deal through:

- body language (the way we sit or stand, whether we look at the person and so on)
- gestures
- facial expressions
- tone of voice (for example, enthusiastic, calm, angry, reassuring, tearful, scornful)
- sighing, laughing, yawning, making noises of agreement or disagreement.

You are going to use this framework to help you analyse in more detail the way the discussions in *The Apprentice* work.

■ In your group, each person should choose one contestant to focus on from the two lists below.

Velocity (the women's group): Nargis, Jo, Ruth, Alexa, Karen

Invicta (the men's group): Samuel, Syed, Ansell, Tuan, Paul

■ As you watch the discussions, pay attention to the ways your male and female contestant use body language, tone of voice and other forms of non-verbal communication to get their point across. Record what you notice on the transcripts on page 116-120.

■ Share your notes with the rest of your group.

■ After you have watched the clips, use the transcript and your annotations to complete the chart on page 114. You might find it helpful to work as a group on this part of the task.

■ Using the transcripts, choose an example from *The Apprentice* to illustrate each of the features of a discussion.

■ Write two or three sentences describing anything that particularly strikes you about the body language and tone of voice used by any of the contestants as they work together. (For example, does body language and tone of voice always confirm what is being said? Do any of the people who stay silent in the discussion reveal what they think and feel through their body language?)

© English and Media Centre, 2008     LANGUAGE WORKS     **113**

# Framework 3 – Non-Verbal Communication

| Name | Example of non-verbal communication | What this communicates |
|---|---|---|
| Nargis | | |
| Jo | | |
| Ruth | | |
| Alexa | | |
| Karen | | |
| Samuel | | |
| Syed | | |
| Ansell | | |
| Tuan | | |
| Paul | | |

THE APPRENTICE

## Sharing Groups

■ Take it in turns to feedback each group has discovered about the way Velocity and Invicta work together:

- Framework 1: roles taken in the discussion
- Framework 2: features of the discussion (conversation analysis)
- Framework 3: non-verbal communication

# Re-wind

## Re-writing the Script

In analysing the way the groups worked together you may have noticed some things which were not very effective or could have been done differently. Now is your chance to have a go at taking the discussion in a different direction.

You are going to work in groups of five on the following extract: Velocity 1: from 'Jo: Tell me how this relates to children then' to 'Jo wiggling fingers in the air to get attention'. The contestants involved in this discussion are: Nargis, Jo, Alexa, Ruth, Sharon. Share out the roles in your group.

■ Read the extract out loud, as a drama script. (If you have nothing to say, think about how you might be using non-verbal communication to take part in the discussion and make your feelings known.)

■ Share your response to the discussion and the way the group is working together at this point. Could the discussion have developed in a different way? How could Jo have got her point across in a positive way? What could Nargis, the group leader, have done to make Jo feel she was being listened to?

■ Experiment with role-playing different ways the group could have discussed this tricky disagreement.

■ Listen to one or two of the role-plays and share your ideas about the strategies which seem most successful.

■ Sum up what you have learned about the way discussions work when people with different ideas are working together to get something done. Choose two points that you think help a group work well together (for example, taking turns) and two points that you think make it hard for a group to work well together. You could use the prompts below to get you started. Be ready to feed back in sharing groups or whole class discussion.

> When working in a group, it is helpful to ..............
>
> Groups that work well together, tend to ..............
>
> When working in a group, it is not helpful to ..............
>
> Groups that don't work well together, tend to ..............

■ As a class draw up a list of advice for working effectively in groups.

# How Groups Talk

## Planning the Great Ormond Street Calendar – Transcripts

### Women's Group 1

*(unclear voices in the background including Jo: 'wanted to apply that now')*

**Nargis:** why don't we just actually go straight to deciding a theme I think

*(unclear voices in the background)*

**Nargis:** let's decide on a theme straightaway so turn over to the next

**Ruth:** which one did you just click on...

**Jo:** I'm getting confused I don't actually know which one we're deciding on

**Nargis:** we're deciding on what theme we're going to use (.) are we going to use cats and dogs (2) my first choice would be cats

**??:** and mine

**Alexa:** yes

**Nargis:** that's a question

**Ruth:** people in Birmingham won't be buying it just because it's going to Great Ormond Street they'll be buying it because it's got kittens in there

**Jo:** tell me how this relates to children then

**Nargis:** it's the ki... cats and dogs that sell the most

**Jo:** cute cats don't do it for me

**Ruth:** but the team are actually making that decision (.) so how can it be wrong if the team are making the decision

**Jo:** I think we need to be more creative

**Sharon:** the negativity and the fact that when we go forward you take us back is actually wasting a lot of our time here.

**Karen?:** it is wasting a lot of our time

**Sharon:** and a lot of our energy

**Jo:** *(wiggling fingers in the air to get attention)*

**Sharon:** your points of view are very valuable right em but we really need to move on and we need

**Jo:** can I just say one word

**Sharon:** need to agree...

**Jo:** I don't really fundamentally believe in the stylish cats and dogs I think it's bollocks

**Nargis:** we've heard you say that (.) now as a team the rest of us have decided to go with this (2) are you going to play

**Jo:** what what do you think what that really pisses me (.) what do you think I am going to do

**??:** yeah

**Karen:** we've just got to draw a line under it and say I said no and if it all goes tits up you can hold your

# The Apprentice

        hand up and say I did that

**Sharon:** did my best to try to persuade them

**Karen:** however you have to be able to show you are 100% on board

**Jo:** to my mind we should be having some feel in there about what Great Ormond Street says you know I mean I was thinking that we should get in contact with some of the flipping kids that have survived from here and and we do tell some stories

*(Unclear mutterings from a number of other people)*

**??:** I can't see

**Jo:** I tell you what I tell you what I've got a friend I know this they've sent me a card in the post and some of you have seen it that's got a child with heart problems and she would love to put her little story on it and I know because she tells me that don't

**Nargis:** we had discussed this earlier and we've been through all of this

**Ruth:** and that's why

**Nargis:** that's why we've decided on cats

## Men's Group 1

**Samuel:** so just keep an eye on time as we're going through the day that will really help (.) and if we're wandering

*(programme edited)*

**Samuel:** anyone disagrees with anything, just speak up

**??:** yeah you know

*(some unclear comments)*

**Samuel:** we're doing this in case we've missed something

**Samuel:** I just want to make a point about something right, just in terms of brainstorming and er coming up with ideas so (.) erm (.) one way you can brainstorm ideas is we can just all have a free for all (.) so you can brainstorm ideas, right, all over the shop ok and you might hit, here's your target ok and you might hit the target and you might not (.) the second way em that you can brainstorm (.) brainstorm criteria er filter

**Syed:** I think simplicity is the way forward you know all we need to is decide on a theme now can we not just

**Samuel:** no I'm just

**Syed:** you need a process

**Samuel:** no let's just have

**Ansell:** we need to come up with 13 we've got just 5 we're not moving on now (.) we need to get these down.

*(Tuan: speaks to camera, commenting on the way the group is working together)*

**Samuel:** so we can start (.) we can get a headstart on the brainstorm and still carry on at 7pm

**Ansell:** I'm going to time everybody (.) I'm going to give everybody one minute (.) I would suggest just one minute to get your ideas down cos there's no discussion about this about the ideas it's just bam bam bam bam

**Tuan:** can you just... it's what we're negotiating (.) this is what we're talking about

**Ansell:** you're not discussing why (.) you're just getting it out

**Samuel:** the obvious strategy is to go with babies

**??:** yeah hence the reason why

# THE APPRENTICE

**Women's Group 2**

**Nargis:** OK are we all in (.) Jo (.) can you come (.) come and join in

**Jo:** well I need to finish about this plastic (?) card so I'm just having a look a little look see if I can find anything

**??:** Jo Jo

**Jo:** *unclear*

*(unclear background noises)*

**Nargis:** one decision that's made is the calendar's going to be extremely cute (*background: simple*) and extremely simple stylish and chic (.) that's what we're doing

**??:** yes

**??:** that's the vision

**Nargis:** the rest

**Jo:** stylish contemporary (.) no big mistake

**Michelle:** we're talking about (.) white backgrounds fairly modern fairly different

**Ruth:** different shots natural

**Michelle:** we're going to play (.) we're going to have action

**Alexa:** it's subtle (*noise/comments in the background*) it's stylish

**Jo:** that is a Great Ormond Street publication right (.) that is not white and contemporary (.) that is bright in your face and a little guy on there (.) it's not bri it's not cute cats

**Karen:** you are a bit pissed off cos it's not what you want but actually you have to say

**Jo::** I just think it's the wrong decision for the team to take

**Karen:** well, I know but it's too late for that Jo (.) you have to come on board

**Sharon:** Jo any opinion

**Karen:** you have to come on board

**Nargis:** contemporary timeless classic that's why we're doing that you are going with it

**??:** yeah

*(unclear background noises)*

**Nargis:** that's it final

*(unclear background noises)*

**Nargis:** final that's it

**??:** yeah

**Ruth:** we've all made a decision

**??:** let's just move on the next bit and start working on

## How Groups Talk

**Men's Group 2**

**??:** I'm just going to have

**??:** perfect

**Syed:** this baby's going to be a doctor this baby's going to be a business man this baby's going to be an astronaut and em and actually dress em up and all this

*(unclear comments in the background)*

**Samuel:** so the first shot let's agree the first shot which is business baby right (.) Tuan you alright with this

**Tuan:** yeah yeah

**Samuel:** you keeping up

**Tuan:** yeah get on with it get on with it

**Samuel:** that's the first one

**??:** hand

**Samuel:** doctor

**??:** astronaut

**Tuan:** astronaut baby

**Samuel:** that's brickie

**Tuan:** brickie baby

**Ansell?:** that's wicked really good

*(in the background: yeah just what else)*

**THE APPRENTICE**

# Year 9 Apprentices

A group of Year 9 boys from Seven Kings School in London took part in the calendar planning activity. Like Alan Sugar's apprentices, they began by choosing a name for their group, then went on to plan their calendar and make their presentation.

Hassan

Kulraj

Wesley

Waqar

Umar

© English and Media Centre, 2008

## Year 9 Apprentices – Planning the Calendar

- Remind yourself of what you have learned about the way groups work together through watching the contestants on *The Apprentice*.

  In role as observers, you are going to watch the way the boys work together. Your task is to identify both the strengths of the group and any areas which you felt could be improved. You should pay attention to:

  - the way the boys work together
  - how they build on each other's ideas
  - how they disagree with each other
  - how they reach a decision
  - the different roles the boys take (for example is there a clear leader or do different boys take this role at different points in the discussion?).

- Feed back your observations in whole class discussion. For any area of weakness, suggest as many strategies as you can which would help the group improve the way they work together in the future.

- In pairs, use your own observations and the ideas raised in class discussion to give some written feedback.

  One of the group's strengths was ................................................................

  ..............................................................................................................

  An area which I felt needed improvement was ........................................

  ..............................................................................................................

  This is because ......................................................................................

  ..............................................................................................................

  ..............................................................................................................

  To improve the way you work together, you need to ................................

  ..............................................................................................................

  ..............................................................................................................

  Next time you are working together, you could .......................................

  ..............................................................................................................

  ..............................................................................................................

## THE APPRENTICE

### Year 9 Apprentices – Pitching the Idea
The Year 9 boys go on to 'pitch' their idea for a school calendar.

■ Watch the group making their pitch and, as a class, share your response to it, for example was it clear, straightforward, lively, detailed and so on?

Pause the DVD after 'Making the pitch'.

■ In pairs, suggest ways in which the group might make the presentation more effective.

■ Feed back your ideas in class discussion. Your teacher will draw up a class list.

### Re-making the pitch
After pitching their ideas, the boys listened to some advice about how they might improve their presentation and delivered it for a second time.

■ Watch the second presentation, noting down your immediate response to it.

■ Watch this second presentation again, this time making a note of the alterations the boys have made. Some of the changes you could look out for, include:
- content
- length
- organisation, including who participated and how the presentation was shared out
- language used
- delivery (tone, speed, expressions)
- relationship with the listener
- body language.

■ Feed back your observations to the rest of the class and talk about the ways in which the boys improved their presentation. Was there anything which you think made their presentation less effective? If so, why was this?

### Tips for Top Presentations
■ Use what you have learned from watching the two presentations and your own experience to draw up a list of top tips for making a great presentation. For example:
- Make eye contact with your audience.
- Use examples to illustrate what you are saying.

# Simulation – Cash and Choice

This simulation asks you to imagine that your school has been given a substantial sum of money. The Governors and Headteacher have drawn up a shortlist of ten possible options for spending it. They have asked small groups of pupils from the School Council to consider the ten options and to present their recommendations to the Governors.

## Stage A – Discussion and Decision Making

### Observers

- If you are asked to be an 'observer', you will not take part in the simulation but will focus on watching and listening to the way one of the School Council groups works together. Use the chart below to record your observations.

| | |
|---|---|
| Getting started | |
| Keeping on track | |
| Building on each other's ideas | |
| Disagreeing | |
| Reaching a decision | |
| The roles different group members take (for example leader, organiser, listener) | |
| Overall strengths | |
| Something to be worked at | |
| Any other comments | |

# THE APPRENTICE

**School Council Groups**

■ In role as members of the School Council, discuss the ten options for how the money should be spent, weighing up the advantages and disadvantages of each. Agree which option you will be recommending and note the reasons for your choice.

> 1. Free school trip abroad for everyone in the current Year 9
> 2. A new tuck shop and a free tea and coffee machine in every classroom
> 3. A common room area for your year group
> 4. A laptop for all students currently doing GCSE
> 5. A makeover of the classrooms, with new paint and carpets
> 6. Free instrumental lessons for anyone who wants them
> 7. A weights training facility
> 8. A dedicated drama studio
> 9. A sponsorship programme in music, art, drama and sport to allow students to have professional training
> 10. A recording studio

■ Write a slogan which will persuade the teachers and pupils to support your choice.

■ Plan a 2-minute presentation to the Governors, making sure you clearly explain the reasons for your choice. Use your 'Tips for Top Presentations' to make sure you get your ideas across clearly and persuasively. Be prepared to answer questions from the Governors and Headteacher.

## Stage B – The Presentations

When not making your own presentation you will play the part of the Governors, able to question each group about what they have chosen to spend their money on.

■ Take it in turns to make your presentation to the Governors and to answer their questions.

## Stage C – Reflecting on Group Work

■ Share some of your thoughts about the way you worked as a group, then listen to the feedback from the observers.

■ On your own, write two or three sentences, summing up how well you think you have worked as a group. What were your strengths? Is there anything you think you could improve on next time? Use the sentence starters on page 122 to help you organise your ideas.

■ As a class, use what you have learned from analysing the way groups work together and from taking part in group work yourself, to draw up a 'Good Group Work Guide' for another class.

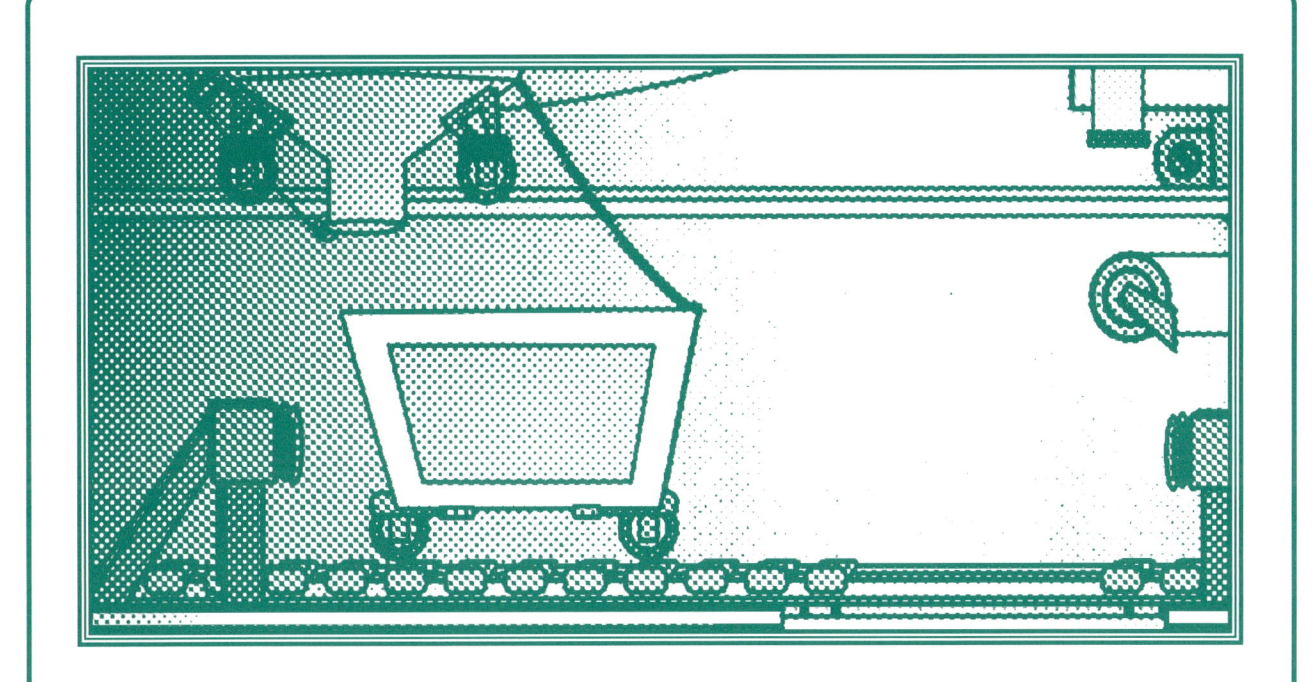

# Cocoa Bean
## Words That Sell

# Teachers' Notes

All the images included in the unit are available as colour pdfs on the DVD.

## DVD Menu

The following activities have a DVD element signalled with this icon: **DVD**

| Selectable section | Duration | Onscreen title | See page |
|---|---|---|---|
| How we got started | 40 secs | | 131 |
| Our packaging | 1 min | | 133 |
| Admiring Innocent | 1 min | | 133 |
| Working on the words | 2 mins 30 | Choosing the right words | 135 |
| | | Standing out from the crowd | |
| | | A close look at language | |
| Wild and Classic | 3 mins | Wild chocolate | 135 |
| | | Classic chocolate | |
| | | Naughty but nice | |
| Inside the packaging | 45 secs | | 137 |

## Additional Resources

Worksheets, colour images, further resources in PDF format included on the DVD are signalled with this icon:

**128** LANGUAGE WORKS © English and Media Centre, 2008

COCOA BEAN

# Words That Sell

**In this unit you will:**
- explore the way verbal language and visual language is used in marketing
- learn in more detail about the way one company uses language to create an image of its product
- experiment with using language to sell a product.

## Painting a Picture, Selling a Product

Some people make their living from advertising. They use words that will persuade people they really can't manage without a particular product – a cereal, snack, chocolate bar or car, for example. They have to use language to get across the image they want to create.

■ Look at the names of products listed here.

| Innocent | Comfort | Sunny Delight |
|---|---|---|
| Vanish | Glade | Mr Sheen |

■ For each one, talk about what type of product you think (or know) is being advertised and why the producers might have decided on this name. Some of the things you might think about are:

- the meaning of the word
- the sound of the word
- associations the word has
- what is being sold.

It's not only the name of the product which is important; it's also the *way* in which the product is described. Printed on page 130 are the top adjectives and verbs used in advertising.

■ You are going to work in pairs on three adjectives and three verbs.

■ Write down your three adjectives and three verbs with plenty of space around them. Use one colour to annotate each word with the associations it has for you. In a second colour, add notes on the type of product you think might use these words.

■ Talk about the advantages and disadvantages of using words which instantly conjure up a particular image in the mind of the customer.

# Words That Sell

**Adjectives**

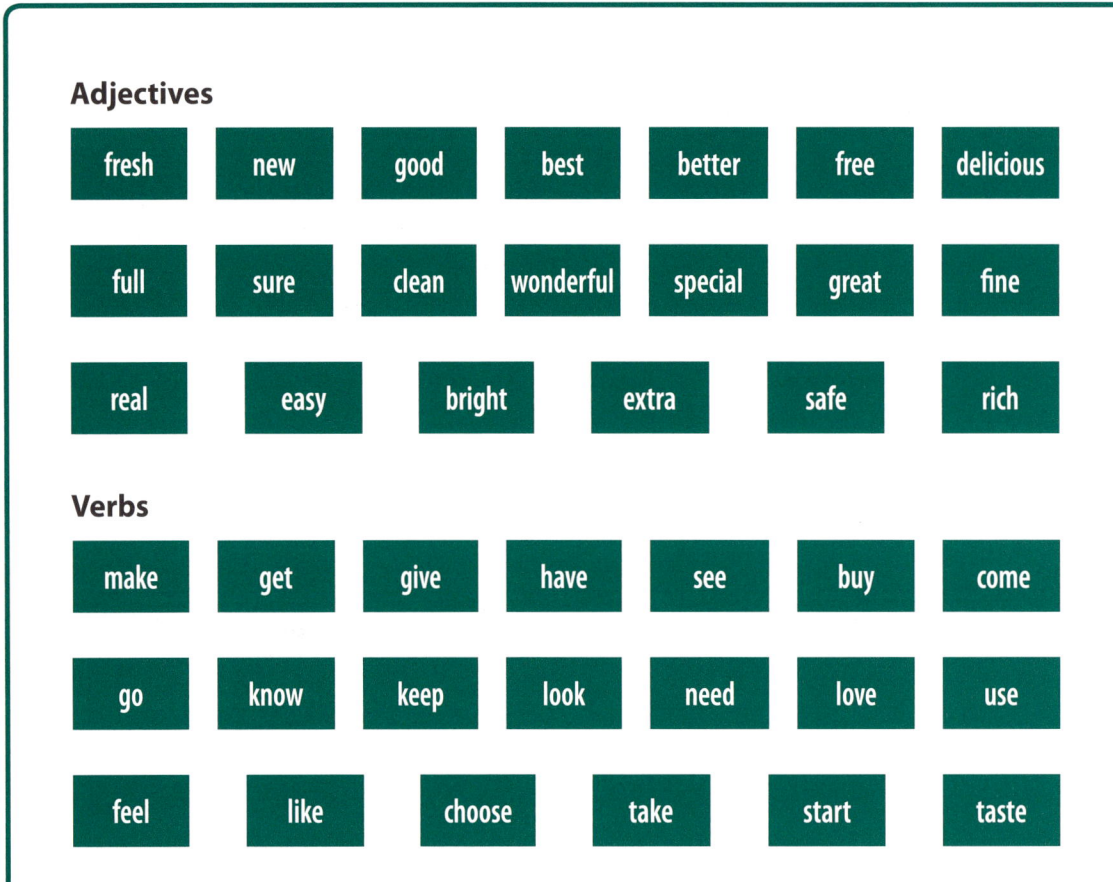

| fresh | new | good | best | better | free | delicious |
| full | sure | clean | wonderful | special | great | fine |
| real | easy | bright | extra | safe | rich |

**Verbs**

| make | get | give | have | see | buy | come |
| go | know | keep | look | need | love | use |
| feel | like | choose | take | start | taste |

## Arresting Language

One of the problems of using too many of these very common descriptions is that customers stop noticing them or they can't remember which product is described by which term.

The producers and their advertisers are constantly trying to think of new ways to use language imaginatively so that their customers notice and remember their product. The car manufacturer Nissan based a whole advertising campaign around the invention of a new language: 'Do you speak Micra?' it asked the audience, before going on to define the new words invented to describe the car:

'modtro' – modern yet retro

'simpology' – simple technology

'spafe' – spontaneous yet safe

You are going to have a go at using language inventively to help get a product noticed.

- Choose a product you know well, for example a drink, a type of trainer or a magazine.

- Without thinking too much, write notes on the qualities and characteristics of the product. For example a trainer might be comfortable, cool or well-fitting.

- Take the words you have written down and experiment with inventing new words to describe the product (perhaps by blending two words or by choosing a word which sounds good or which has a slang meaning as well as its standard meaning).

- Take it in turns to read out your words, without mentioning the product and see if the rest of the class can guess what you are describing.

Cocoa Bean

# Cocoa Bean Case Study

Sarah Hehir and Emily Sandford are sisters who, five years ago, set up Cocoa Bean, a company making unusually flavoured dark chocolates. From the very beginning they knew it was important to create the right impression through their use of language in their publicity, on their packaging and in advertising. They spend a long time thinking about just the right word to use and over the years have changed the way they describe their company and their chocolates.

## How We Got Started

■ Watch Emily and Sarah on the DVD as they introduce themselves and their company.

## The Early Days

Included on page 132 are examples of Cocoa Bean's labels and packaging from 2002, when Sarah and Emily were still making the chocolates in their kitchen and selling them at a local food market. (Colour versions of these images are available on the DVD.)

■ In pairs, talk about your first impressions of these labels. You should think about:

- design
- colour
- fonts
- words used to describe the company
- words used to describe the chocolates
- the impression you get of the company and of the chocolates.

Emily describes their chocolates as:

'very bold and innovative. We specialise in dark chocolate flavoured with fresh natural ingredients, very exciting unusual flavours.'

■ Use the chart below to summarise your views about whether or not the early packaging manages to get this across to the customer.

■ How would *you* use words, images, font, colour and so on to communicate what Sarah and Emily think is important about Cocoa Bean? On your own or in pairs, brainstorm all your ideas.

| Successful | Not Successful |
|---|---|
|  |  |

© English and Media Centre, 2008     LANGUAGE WORKS     **131**

# Words That Sell

## Examples of Labels and Packaging from 2002

---

**COCOA BEAN
HANDMADE TRUFFLES**

DELICIOUSLY DARK CHOCOLATES WITH
SOFT TRUFFLE CENTRES
HANDMADE IN LIMERICK
TEN DISTINCT FLAVOURS AVAILABLE TO ORDER
DAIRY FREE
CONTACT. SARAH: 061 458907

---

**COCOA BEAN HANDMADE CHOCOLATES**
Luxury truffles - dark and dairy free

Orange ~ dusted with gold
Chocolate ~ a dark chocolate truffle
Raspberry ~ dusted with pink shimmer
Hazelnut ~ topped with roasted hazelnut
Earl Grey Tea ~ with chocolate squiggles
Coffee ~ topped with a real coffee bean
Spice ~ sprinkled with chilli
Apricot ~ topped with a slice of apricot
Rose ~ with a real rose petal
Turkish Delight ~ dark chocolate squares
After Dinner Discs ~ mint discs with chopped almonds

Sarah Webster (061) 458 907

---

**CONFERENCES AND CORPORATE GIFTS**

Cocoa Bean fresh truffles are handcrafted locally using only the finest and freshest of ingredients providing a unique and memorable gift for your client or guest.

Whether you choose to serve truffles with coffee during a conference, after a banquet or function, as a ladies gift or in the guest's suite, you can be assured that the quality of Cocoa Bean chocolates will enhance the image of your company.

We offer personalised labelling, providing the opportunity to advertise the name of your company or mark an event or occasion.

We can provide corporate gifts and cater for conferences and events on any scale.

## Cocoa Bean

### Cocoa Bean Packaging

Soon after launching Cocoa Bean as a business, Sarah and Emily decided to re-design the labelling and packaging to bring it more in line with the 'personality' of their chocolates. (In advertising products are often seen to have a 'personality' like people, for instance bold and imaginative.)

- Watch Sarah and Emily talking about the importance of the packaging in creating the right impression of their chocolate and company.

- Pull out the two points you think are most important or most interesting in what they say. Compare your points with one or two people in your class.

### Admiring Innocent

One of the companies Emily and Sarah particularly admire is Innocent which produces fruit juices and smoothies without additives or artificial ingredients.

- Before hearing what Emily and Sarah have to say, spend two or three minutes studying the example of an Innocent packet on page 134.
    - What's your first response to Innocent's packaging?
    - What impression do you get of the company and its product? What suggests this to you?
    - What message do you think Innocent is trying to get across to customers through its packaging?
    - What type of person do you think the company is trying to attract? Why?

- Now watch the DVD clip to hear what Emily and Sarah admire or find effective about Innocent's packaging.

Some of the language and design features Sarah and Emily highlight include:
- clear logo
- images
- informal language
- chatty
- 1st person
- bold claims

- Use these features to help you annotate the smoothie packaging on page 134. You might also look at the use of:
    - jokes, word play and other forms of humour
    - characters
    - anything else that catches your attention.

For each feature you identify, add an explanation of how it works to create a particular impression of the product – and persuade the shopper to buy it!

## Words That Sell

**Innocent Smoothie Packaging**

### an innocent story

Since we started making smoothies 8 years ago, quite a bit has changed. We started off with 3 recipes, but now we make about 13. These days you can buy us in a lot more shops. And there are loads more people working at Fruit Towers (we recently had to install a fourth toaster to help ease mid-afternoon kitchen congestion).

But we're still run by the same 3 friends who started things in 1999. And we're still making drinks that taste good and do you good. Thanks for helping us get this far. Here's to the next 8 years.

Our eighth birthday cake. Happy birthday to us.

TM = Toast Moments

038862 330602

### innocent™
pure fruit smoothie

**cranberries & raspberries**

never, ever from concentrate

### an innocent promise

We promise that innocent smoothies will always taste good and do you good. We promise that we'll never use this stuff:

NO concentrates   NO preservatives
NO stabilisers    NO added sugar
NO flavourings    NO E numbers
NO GM stuff       NO funny business

And if we do you can tell our mums.

250ml

AT LEAST 2 PORTIONS OF LOVELY FRUIT
OVER 100% RDA OF NATURAL VITAMIN C
100% PURE AND FRESH FRUIT - NEVER, EVER FROM CONCENTRATE

### so what's in the box?

we pressed 9 of these
we mashed 2 of these
we crushed 50 of these
we squeezed 2 of these
we squashed 247 of these
and we didn't add any of these

All of our bananas come from Rainforest Alliance Certified™ plantations. The Rainforest Alliance champions farm workers' rights and promotes positive growing practices that benefit ecosystems and encourage biodiversity. We love them.

COCOA BEAN

### New Packaging

During 2006 Sarah and Emily worked hard on developing the packaging for their chocolate 'Stacks' (10 squares of different flavoured chocolate piled into a tower).

You can see the packaging for the stacks (laid flat) on page 136.

- In pairs, share your first impressions of Cocoa Bean's Stacks. How does this packaging compare with other chocolate wrappers and boxes you are familiar with? If you can, have a look at some examples online.

- Make a note of any similarities and differences in the way Cocoa Bean and the other company use language (including the visual language of colour, images and fonts). For example whereas Cadbury Dairy Milk is mainly purple, Cocoa Bean stacks use lots of different colours.

### Working on the Words

Sarah and Emily both stress the important role language plays in creating the right image of the chocolates.

- Watch the DVD and write down one point that you find interesting about the way language is used on the packaging. Be ready to share your ideas and explain the reason for your choice.

### Wild and Classic

One of the changes Sarah and Emily made was to make and sell two different 'collections' of stacks which they called Wild and Classic.

- In pairs, brainstorm all the meanings and associations of either wild or classic. Your teacher will tell you which word to work on. Join up with a pair who have looked at the other word. Share your ideas. Why do you think Sarah and Emily might have chosen these names for their collections? What impression do you think they trying to convey through the names?

- Watch Sarah and Emily talking about the Wild and Classic stacks and why they chose these names. How do they compare with your thoughts?

### Looking More Closely

- Use your notes on the meanings of wild and classic plus any new ideas from the interview to annotate the packaging of one of the collections.

- Look back at the features Sarah and Emily identified as effective on the Innocent Smoothie packaging. Which features have they used or adapted for the Wild and Classic stacks?

- Choose one feature from the 'Stacks' packaging which you think works well and explain why. Then either choose a feature which you think is less effective and explain how you would change it, or suggest a new technique Cocoa Bean could use on its packaging.

# WORDS THAT SELL

## cocoabean WILD CHOCOLATE

Flavours:
- Fire
- Spice
- Lime & Black Pepper
- 99%
- Gin & Tonic
- Wild Flower
- Irish Honey
- Sea Salt
- Rose & Pistachio
- Star Anise & Ginger

With a devilish flair for creating ruinously addictive chocolate, the **cocoa**bean chocolatiers combine their slavish search for radical flavours with cocoa sourced from small plantations across the world.

The Wild Collection is for the super-tasters who happily suck on salt crystals and cheerfully crunch peppercorns. They like change, they like most things, but most of all they like their chocolate to pack a punch.

**Fire** Chipotle chillies, pink peppercorns, essence of oak.

**Spice** Cardamom, root ginger, tickle of chilli.

**Wild Flower** Rose, lavender, orange blossom honey from Valencia.

**Irish Honey** From Glenanore Apiaries, Co Cork. Sweet honey with 85% cocoa hit.

**99%** Some people claim chocolate this strong is illegal. It's not, yet.

**Gin & Tonic** Crushed juniper berries and fresh lime zest.

**Sea Salt** 60% chocolate and Maldon sea salt.

**Lime & Black Pepper** **Rose & Pistachio** **Star Anise & Ginger** are all exactly what they say they are.

All zest freshly grated. Spices freshly crushed or ground for each batch.

All the chocolate is 72% unless otherwise stated.

## cocoabean CLASSIC CHOCOLATE

Flavours:
- Earl Grey Tea
- Ginger
- Orange
- Cinnamon
- Mint
- Espresso
- Hazelnut
- Nutmeg

With an unparalleled flair for creating ruinously addictive chocolate, **cocoa**bean blends bold flavours with chocolate sourced from small, dedicated producers across the world.

"It doesn't take much to see that the problems of three little people don't amount to a hill of beans in this crazy world." Humphrey Bogart, Casablanca

The flavours in the Classic Collection are exactly what they say they are. Oranges are freshly zested to make chocolates that taste of oranges. The ginger chocolate tastes of ginger because that is what's in it. And rather than mix coffee flavour into our espresso bar we stud it with espresso roast coffee beans so you can choose when to release the hit of great coffee into the rich mouthful of pure dark chocolate.

These are classic flavours. Don't mess.

## Cocoa Bean

### Inside the Packaging

Included here is an example of the *inside* of Cocoa Bean packaging. (A colour version is included on the DVD.)

■ Study the packaging and share your first responses, before thinking further about the following points:

- the use of pictures (sometimes in place of letters, for example the bean instead of the 'o' in 'so')
- the font
- the images
- the arrangement of words and images on the page
- the way the reader is addressed
- information about the ingredients, where they come from and how the chocolates are made
- information about the company.

■ Watch Sarah explain why they decided to use the inside of the packaging in this way. Do you think they have been successful? In pairs, talk about any further ideas you have for how Cocoa Bean could use the inside of the packaging.

## All Change!

Now's your chance to explore practically the way the language and design work together to create a particular impression and impact. On page 139 you will find the written text from inside the Wild Stack packaging and the individual images. The text as a Word file and the individual images are included on the DVD.

- On sheets of plain paper, experiment with changing different elements of the design (the appearance of the text, the colours, layout, the images and so on) to see what different impression you create.

- What happens if you use a computer rather than handwriting for the text? Do different fonts create a different impression?

- So far you've been working with Cocoa Bean's text and images. You might have other ideas about how they could describe the chocolates, tell the consumer the story of Cocoa Bean and the way the chocolate is made and so on.

- Try re-writing the text in your own words. You might decide to miss out some of the text altogether or get the ideas across using images rather than words.

- When you have experimented with several different versions, create a final version of the Wild Stack's inside packaging using the template below.

*Space for you to create your own Wild Stack inside*

## Cocoa Bean

Why is our chocolate so good?

Only cocoa butter

No vegetable oils or cheap substitutes

www.cocoabeanchocolates.com

Only use dark stuff! Richer more complex flavours

Noble ingredients award

Blended in Paris by family firm with 50 years experience

Careful roasting ensures rich flavour, not bitter like some hurriedly roasted commercial chocolate

= a great healthy evening

More anti-oxidants than red wine

Grown to organic principles fully traceable and ethically traded

All flavours natural, freshly grated, ground and zested

Beans are conched for a whole week for a gorgeous smooth texture

Turning beans into chocolate takes ages

Contains just cocoa solids, cocoa butter, cane sugar and madagascan vanilla beans

Cocoa butter melts at body temperature

That's why it's so sexy because it melts in the mouth

Grown by experts harvested at the perfect time for a deeper flavour not in commercial drying houses

# Words That Sell

# Simulation

## Marketing Cocoa Bean Lollipops

Imagine Cocoa Bean has decided to create and market a lollipop for children. This lollipop must be attractive to children but must also appeal to the adult who decides what the children can eat and has the money to buy it. Innocent Smoothies has already tackled this issue with their Innocent Smoothies for Kids.

- Look closely at the Smoothie for Kids cartons below. You can see colour versions of these images on the DVD.

- In pairs, talk about the ways in which words, images, layout, colours and so on are used to appeal to both parents and children.

- Choose one technique or feature you think is effective and explain why it works well.

- Take it in turns to feed back your favourite technique to the rest of the class. Together draw up a list of the top five techniques.

140  LANGUAGE WORKS  © English and Media Centre, 2008

COCOA BEAN

## Lollipop Label – Role-Play (groups of three)

**Stage 1 – Chocolate Company Groups: Product Development Manager, Chocolatier and Designer (see role-cards on page 142)**

> **The brief:**
> Design a label for the chocolate lollipop that will appeal to both parents and children.

> **The product:**
> Dark chocolate lollipops, described on the Cocoa Bean website as:
>> These chunky circles of fabulous dark chocolate blended with herbs, spices and fruits are great stirred through hot chocolate. (Cinnamon, Spice, Bourbon Vanilla (60%), Mint, Orange, Chocolate, Hazelnut)

> **Key product information:**
> - less sugar in it than many commercial chocolates
> - no artificial flavours, colourings, preservatives in them
> - solid chocolate with exciting/weird/unusual flavours
> - contains iron
> - antioxidants
> - range of flavours
> - brightly coloured wrappings
> - grown to organic principles
> - careful roasting means there is no bitterness in the chocolate
> - handmade
> - hand wrapped

- ■ In your threes, decide which of you will play the part of Product Development Manager, Chocolatier and Designer. Read the role-cards on page 142.

- ■ In role, brainstorm what ideas you want to get across to both parents and children. Choose the information you are going to include on the labels on the front and back of the lollipop.

- ■ Talk about the way you will use words, metaphors, similes, sounds, jokes, facts, colours and fonts to present your product in a way that appeals to both parents and children.

- ■ Experiment with different ways of combining text and images to create the impression you want to get across.

- ■ When you are happy with your design, use the templates on page 143 to draft your label. This can be quite sketchy, with notes indicating the colours, images and so on you would use.

- ■ You now need some feedback on your packaging. You are going to give your ideas to another group who will comment on your ideas from the point of view of a child, a parent and a buyer (the person who decides what a supermarket will stock).

**Role cards for Stage 1 (instructions on page 141)**

> **Role card 1: Product Development Manager**
>
> Your job is to:
>
> develop new ranges and target new markets
>
> work with the chocolatier on developing new flavours and products
>
> set out for the designer what you want from the packaging
>
> make sure that the packaging is truthful and legal, as well as enticing

> **Role card 2: Chocolatier**
>
> Your job is to:
>
> experiment with new flavours and textures for chocolates
>
> sum up what it is about the chocolate that needs highlighting in the packaging
>
> suggest colours, images, text that the designer and copywriter might use in the packaging

> **Role card 3: Designer and copywriter**
>
> Your job is to:
>
> listen to the Product Development Manager and Chocolatier about the chocolates they have created and who they are aimed at
>
> experiment with language, colours, images, fonts and so on to find a way of reflecting what the chocolate is like in the packaging

### Stage 2 – Feedback Groups: Children, Parents and Buyers

In your groups of three you are now going to act as the feedback panel for another group, responding to their packaging in role as either a parent, child or buyer for a big food chain. Your teacher will tell you which role to play.

- In role as parent, child or buyer, share your first responses to the packaging you have been given to comment on. Then talk in more detail about the way language and design has been used to meet the brief. Together draft a short piece of written feedback, summing up the strengths of the packaging and offering suggestions for how it might be improved.

### Stage 3 – The Re-draft

- Read the report you have been given by your feedback panel and make any alterations to your lollipop design in the light of their comments.

## Cocoa Bean

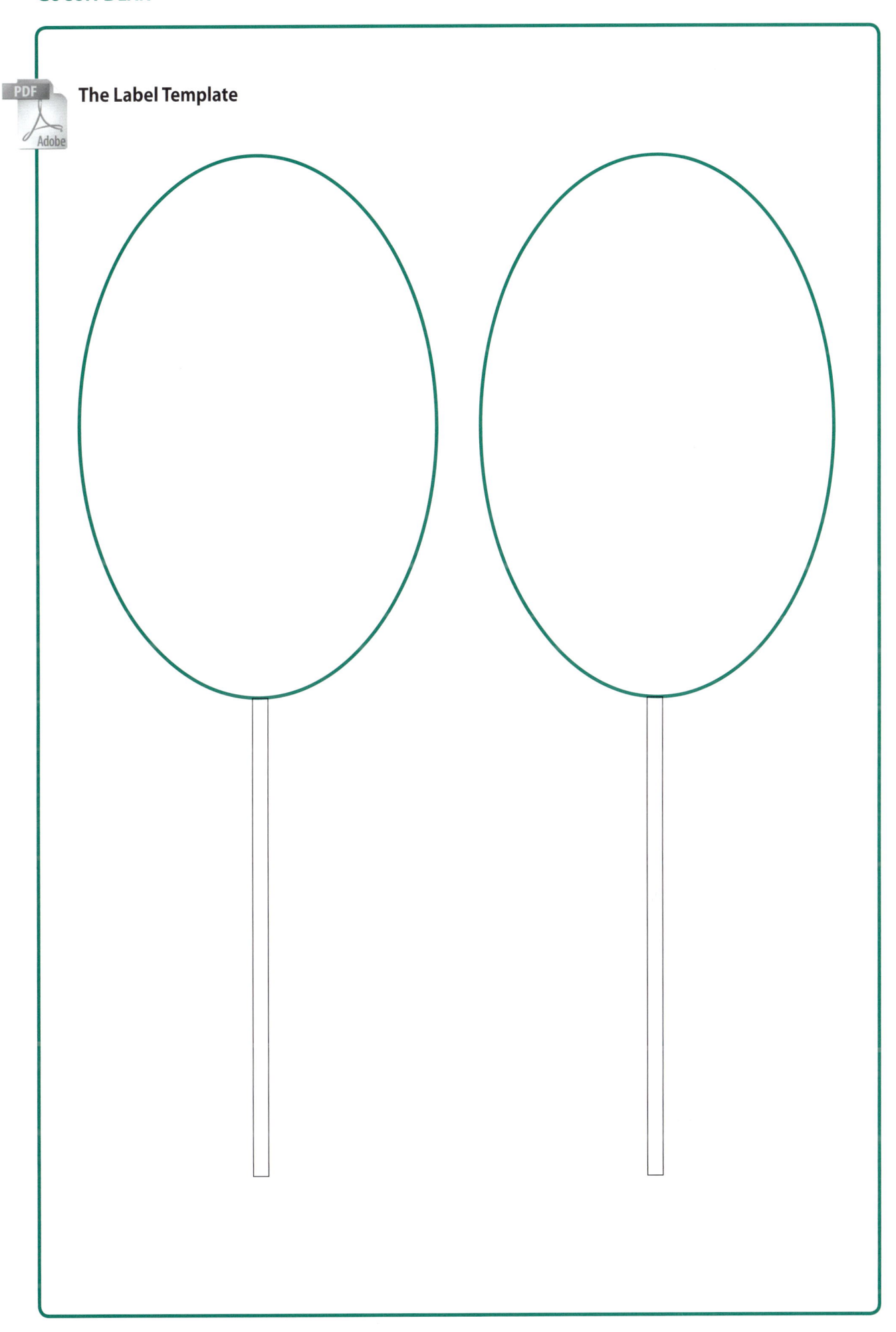

**The Label Template**

© English and Media Centre, 2008

WORDS THAT SELL

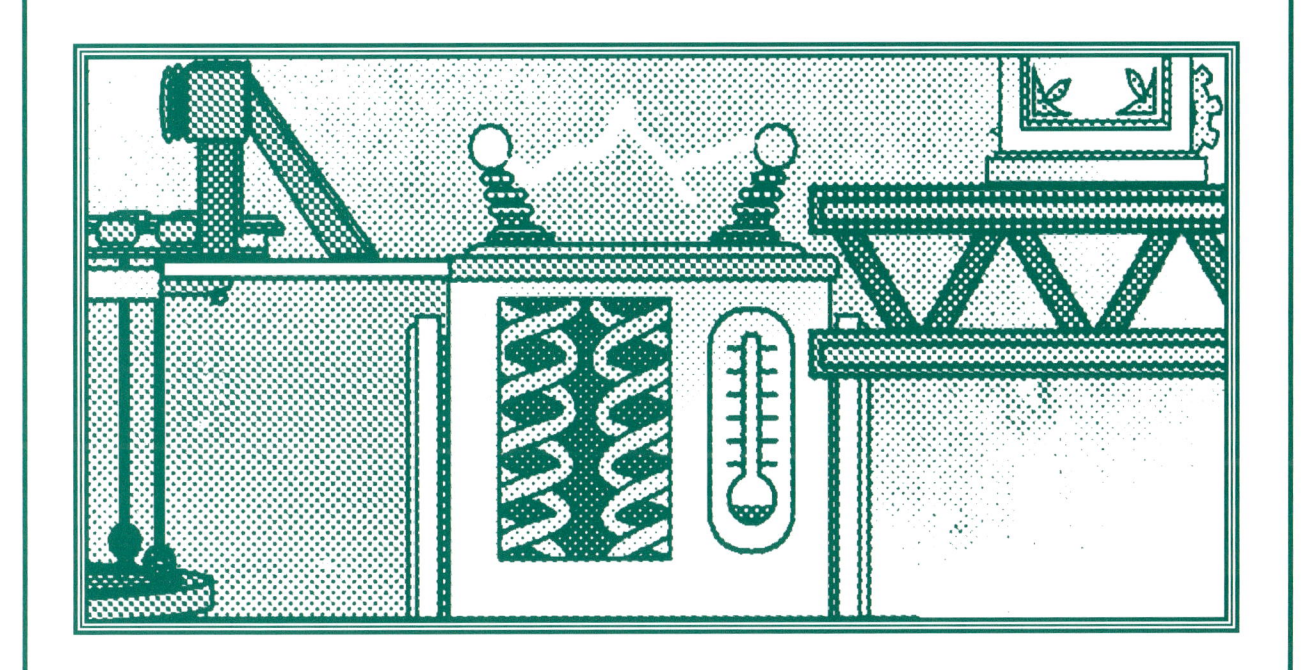

# What's Cool?

## Digging for Words

# Teachers' Notes

## DVD Menu

The following activities have a DVD element signalled with this icon: **DVD**

| Selectable section | Duration | Onscreen title | See page |
|---|---|---|---|
| Where 'cool' comes from | 11 mins 30 | | 151 |

WHAT'S COOL?

# How Language Changes

**In this unit you will:**
- explore some of the ways in which the English language has changed
- learn about the origins of the word 'cool' and the way its meaning has changed
- carry out a mini-investigation into different words for 'good'.

## Investigating the Ways Words Change

Here are some different ways that words appear in the language and the ways they change.

**1. Words are borrowed from other languages**

| Word | Language |
| --- | --- |
| Vodka | Russian |
| Pyjamas | Persian |
| Umbrella | Italian |
| Yoghurt | Turkish |
| Slogan | Gaelic |

| Word | Language |
| --- | --- |
| Chocolate | Nahuatl |
| Judo | Japanese |
| Restaurant | French |
| Sugar | Arabic |
| Guitar | Spanish |

■ Try using a good dictionary to investigate where these words come from:

| Word | Language |
| --- | --- |
| Patio | |
| Magazine | |
| Shampoo | |
| Karaoke | |
| Jazz | |
| Discotheque | |
| Poodle | |
| Robot | |
| Dungarees | |
| Thug | |
| Microphone | |
| Alcohol | |

## 2. Words and phrases are lost from the language

Whatever happened to these words and phrases?

> Drasty – filthy (In the 14th Century, Chaucer talks of 'drasty rhyming'.)
>
> Drovy – muddy (Another word used by Chaucer.)
>
> Wlonk – proud (Used in the Middle Ages.)
>
> Scobberlotcher – someone wandering round lost in thought. (Originally used in 16th century for an undergraduate walking round a quad, lost in thought and/or counting trees!)
>
> Snite his snitch – hit him on the nose (Originally used in the 17th century meaning 'wipe his nose, or give him a good flap on the face'.)

■ Can you think of any words or phrases from the past that are no longer used, for example 'winklepickers' (pointy-toed shoes 50s), 'Blighty' for England (before and during 2nd World War), 'LP' (long playing vinyl record)?

## 3. Words can change their meanings by becoming wider or narrower in meaning.

In the 16th century, 'mete' meant 'food' – now it means just one kind of food.

'Virtue' once applied only to men – now it includes women as well.

## 4. Words can also develop more positive or negative connotations.

Words which become more positive over time are said to ameliorate, while words which become more negative are said to pejorate.

'Hussy' once just meant 'housewife'. It later became an insulting word to use about women.

'Wicked' once meant evil. Now it can have a positive connotation.

These changes can tell us something about changing attitudes in society, or changing ways of life.

■ See if you can complete the chart on page 149, ticking the column that shows how the word has changed. If none of the types of change seem relevant, try and describe in your own words how the word has changed.

## What's Cool?

| Word and its old meaning | How it is used now ||||
|---|---|---|---|---|
| | Wider | Narrower | Ameliorated | Pejorated |
| Silly once meant happy | | | | |
| A butcher once meant a killer of goats | | | | |
| Harlot once meant a young man | | | | |
| In the Bible bread meant all kinds of food | | | | |
| Vulgar once meant ordinary | | | | |
| A doctor was once used for any learned man | | | | |
| A villain was once a farm labourer | | | | |
| Naughty once meant worthless | | | | |
| Awesome once meant impressive and frightening | | | | |

5. **Words are often invented to fill a gap in the language**

This can be done by:

- **blending** two existing words, for example smog is a blend of fog and smoke; brunch is a blend of breakfast and lunch, podcast is a blend of iPod and broadcast
- by using a **trade or brand name**: Thermos, Hoover, Sellotape, Blu-tak and Biro are all trade names that were used for new products, which came to be used for all examples of that product
- by **linking words**, for example Blog links two words (web and log) to make a new one
- by using **initials** or **acronyms**, for example Radar and Scuba were each originally acronyms for a longer phrase
- by **changing the function of a word**, for example text was once just a noun (a text) but is now also a verb (to text)
- by **borrowing** bits of other words, for example Hyper, Mega, Super and Multi are all prefixes used to add to the beginnings of words, as in supermarket, or hyperactive

■ Come up with a list of as many examples as you can of words that have been created in each of these ways.

## Over to You

■ Have you ever thought that there just isn't a word for something? Try making up a few of your own words, using each of these different ways of making words, to fill a gap that you've noticed, for example a blend to describe someone who is vegetarian but will eat fish could be a fishetarian. Or what about Grafneaty as a new brand name for a product that erases grafitti from walls? Or perhaps you could use a prefix to describe a brilliant teacher as in megamiss or supersir.

■ Share them as a class, or put them up on display on your classroom wall.

## 'McJob' – challenging the OED

McJob: an unstimulating, low-paid job with few prospects

*Oxford English Dictionary*

In 2007 the *Oxford English Dictionary* (*OED*) included a word which had been gaining popularity. Rather than talking about a low-paid, boring, repetitive or dead-end job, people had begun to talk about 'McJobs'. You can probably guess the origins of this word: the burger chain McDonald's. McDonald's objected to their name being used in such a negative way and began a campaign to get it removed from the dictionary.

■ Work in pairs, with one of you taking the role of spokesperson for the *OED* and one of you taking the role of a McDonald's spokesperson. Put forward the reasons why you think the word 'McJobs' should remain in the dictionary or why it should be removed. Use the points suggested here to start you thinking:

- the use of upper case 'M' and 'J' means that even the look of the word reminds you of McDonald's
- the definition does not link the word to the burger chain
- the OED reflects the way language is being used in society, it doesn't create it
- the OED should not go along with the prejudices of a few people in the society
- 'McJob' is a new word coined to describe a particular sort of low-paid work which has become more common. It is not necessarily connected to the burger chain
- if people use it, it should go in the dictionary.

WHAT'S COOL?

# Becoming a Word Archaeologist

Archaeologists dig down through the soil to find evidence of the past. In this activity, you're going to become a word archaeologist, digging into the past to find out about the origins of words.

You are going to watch a video clip from the TV programme *Balderdash and Piffle*. In this programme, celebrities set themselves the challenge of persuading the writers of the *Oxford English Dictionary* (OED) that their explanations of the origins of a word need to be changed.

In the clip you are going to see, the saxophonist Courtney Pine tries to find out when and why 'cool' started being used to mean more than just 'quite cold', by going to the New York jazz world and tracing the word back to its earliest uses in the American deep South.

## Before Watching

- Brainstorm as many different meanings of the word 'cool' as you can think of.

- Try writing your own dictionary definition for the word 'cool'. Here's an edited version of the dictionary definition of the word 'wet' from the Penguin English Dictionary, which you could use as a model.

> **WET:**
> *adjective* covered or saturated with liquid; rainy; (slang) sentimental; weak, spiritless; (US colloquial) allowing sale of alcohol; wet blanket (colloquial) spoilsport; wet dock – dock with water kept at high-tide level; verb to make wet; drench; wet one's whistle drink
> *noun* moisture; water; rain; (slang) person lacking spirit; sentimental person

*Colloquial* means everyday language.
*Slang* means quirky, unofficial words, often the language of a group rather than the whole society (e.g. teenage slang, prisoners' slang).
*Idioms* are colloquial phrases which mean something different from the literal meaning of the words themselves, for example 'sitting on the fence', 'over the moon' or 'elbow grease'.

- Can you think of any idioms and expressions using the word 'cool'?

## Where 'Cool' Comes From

- Now watch the DVD clip.

## After Watching

- Share what you discovered about the origin and changing meaning of the word 'cool'. Together make a list of bullet points of the most important information, then see if you can number your points to suggest a timescale for the changing uses.

- Adapt your original definition to include anything new that you found out.

## Investigating a Word

Here are some more words that have been used colloquially or in slang to express the idea of excellence at different periods in the history of the language.

| | | |
|---|---|---|
| Groovy | Spiffing | Magic |
| Fab | Far out | Dandy |
| Top notch | Tip-top | Swell |
| Neat | Splendiferous | Extreme |
| Rum | Awesome | Unreal |
| Rad | Mondo | Beaut |
| Wizard | A1 | Fantabulous |
| Ripper | Outasight | |

- Add any other words that you can think of, particularly ones used today.

- Using your own knowledge, annotate the list with first ideas about any of the words. For instance, for a few of them you might have some idea about:
    - when it became a popular word for 'good'
    - in what part of the world it originated (England? Scotland? USA? Australia?)
    - how and why it came to be used to mean 'good'.

# What's Cool?

- Choose one of the words on the list to investigate fully for yourself, using the list of resources below. See if you can find out:
    - *when* it was first used to mean good
    - *where* it was first used to mean good
    - what it originally meant (if it is a word with a long history)
    - how its meaning has changed over time
    - quotations in which it is used, or your own examples of how it is/was used (for instance short examples showing likely phrases or sentences in which it might occur).

Use a range of sources, to find out as much as you can and to check whether the sources agree with each other.

- Produce a small flier (A5 size) about the origins of your word to put up on a big timeline on your classroom wall. You could illustrate your display sheet with a cartoon showing the use of the word in conversation, or other visual images.

As an alternative you could do an oral presentation on your word to the rest of the class.

## Where to Find Out About the Origins of Your Word

### Web
The Oxford English Dictionary Online

urbandictionary.com

worldwidewords.org

A Dictionary of Slang www.peevish.co.uk/slang/links.htm

http://www.aussieslang.com/

### Books
Jonathon Green: *Slang down the Ages*

John Ayto: *Oxford Dictionary of Slang*

*Oxford English Dictionary*

# Digging For Words

**COOKING THE BOOKS**

# COOKING THE BOOKS

## LANGUAGE THROUGH TIME

# Teachers' Notes

## A good choice of texts to compare

**1 and 5 or 6**
These show big differences, in terms of context, overall structure and use of the genre (voice, length, format) and language (lexis, syntax, spelling, use of imperatives, use of the ampersand, punctuation and so on).

**3 and 4**
These are interesting to compare, less because of changes in the recipe format than because of shifts in address to the reader and indications of how the recipes both are influenced by the social context and reveal to us that context. The attitude to ingredients is very different (a moderately affluent household in 1869 compared with austerity cooking during the war), as is the amount of time available for preparing food and the expected consumers of the food (6 to 8 people in a family as compared with the packed lunch in a family where perhaps the man and woman are now both going out to work, or the woman is working in a factory while the man is at war.)

**4 and 6**
These texts are interesting to compare particularly in terms of address to the reader, what the writer thinks the reader may be most interested in, economy of expression and so on. It suggests a very different world of cookery book publishing in the 21st century.

**2 and 5**
There's a huge amount to say about the differences in format, voice, address to the reader, formality and informality, use of lexis, including specialist terminology, use of anecdote and personal details, use of adjectives and so on.

## A First Activity

1. Jamie Oliver: *Happy Days with the Naked Chef*, 2004
2. Nigella Lawson: *Nigella Bites*, 2001
3. *The Good Housekeeping Woman's Home Cook Book (US)*, 1909 (full text not included in the rest of the unit)
4. Nigel Slater: *Toast*, 2004 (full text not included in the rest of the unit)
5. Mrs Beeton: *Book of Household Management*, 1869
6. *Elinor Fettiplace's Receipt Book*, 1604
7. Marguerite Patten: *2nd World War Recipes*, 1940s

## DVD Menu

The following activities have a DVD element signalled with this icon: **DVD**

| Selectable section | Duration | Onscreen title | See page |
| --- | --- | --- | --- |
| Fanny Craddock – 1966 | 4 mins | | 168 |
| Jamie Oliver – 1999 | 4 mins | | 168 |
| Nigella Lawson – 2002 | 4 mins | | 168 |

## Additional Resources

Worksheets, colour images, further resources in PDF format included on the DVD are signalled with this icon:

COOKING THE BOOKS

# Language Through Time

**In this unit you will:**
- explore some of the ways in which the English language has changed
- learn about the connections between language and social change.

## A First Activity

■ Look at the phrases below taken from different texts. What can you tell about the kind of texts each one comes from? Here are some ideas:

- autobiography
- recipe book
- spoken conversation
- radio programme
- health education pamphlet
- encyclopaedia.

■ What helped you make your decision?

1. J_____ has a little drop of Baileys every now and again, so there's usually a bottle hanging about.

2. I go for mostly cream: nothing creates so well that tender-bellied swell of softly set custard.

3. Neatness and order in your pantry will depend in great measure upon the way you clear your table. If you look upon your pantry as a dumping ground, then dirt and disorder will be inevitable, but if on the contrary you consider it a workshop to be shipshape you will avoid these dangers. Shipshape means a place for everything and everything in its place.

4. My mother is buttering bread for England. The vigor with which she slathers soft yellow fat onto thinly sliced white pap is as near as she gets to the pleasure that is cooking for someone you love. Right now she has the bread knife in her hand and nothing can stop her.

5. Butter is indispensable in almost all culinary preparations. Good fresh butter, used in moderation, is easily digested.

6. Take manchet and slice it thin, then take dates the stones cut out, & cut in pieces, & reasins of the Sun the stones puld out, & a few currance.

7. Slices of Bread Pudding are ideal to tuck into a packed meal box for a factory worker.

© English and Media Centre, 2008     LANGUAGE WORKS     **157**

In fact, all of these extracts come from recipe books! Some were written very recently, others a long time ago.

- See if you can match these dates to each extract: 1604, 1869, 1909, 1940s, 2001, 2004, 2004,

- What helped you decide: the ingredients? The words used? The tone of voice? The attitude to food? The spelling? The formality/informality of the style?

## What Recipe Books Used to be Like – a Typical Recipe

Here is a typical recipe from a book written in 1978 by Jane Grigson.

- Annotate it to show typical features of a conventional recipe, for example starting with a list of ingredients.

- For each feature you notice, say what the effect is, for example starting with a list of ingredients allows you to make a list of things to buy, or collect together everything you need before you start.

- Compare what you've discovered with the annotations done for you on page 159.

CREAM OF TURNIP SOUP

350g (12 oz) young turnips, diced

250g (8 oz) potatoes, diced

1 leek or 4 spring onions or 1 medium onion, chopped

2 tablespoons butter

1 tablespoon plain flour

1½ –2 litres (2½ – 3½ pt) stock

salt, black pepper

2 large egg yolks

4 tablespoons whipping or double cream

Cook the vegetables in the butter in a covered pan over a low heat for ten minutes, shake the pan occasionally, or stir the vegetables about, they must not brown. Add the flour, stir again, then moisten gradually, with enough stock to cover the vegetables easily. Season and simmer until the vegetables are tender, from 20-30 minutes.

Blend or sieve the soup through the mouli-legumes, adding enough of the remaining stock to make an agreeable consistency. Return the soup to the pan and reheat gently. Mix the yolks and cream, add a ladleful of hot soup, stirring well, then return to the pan and heat thoroughly for a few moments without boiling. Keep stirring. Taste again for seasoning. Serve with bread croutons.

## Cooking the Books

Typical format with a list of ingredients first, to allow you to collect everything you need.

Numbers and measurements are important – precise language but some trust in the reader's expertise and experience (for example 20-30 minutes).

CREAM OF TURNIP SOUP

350g (12 oz) young turnips, diced

250g (8 oz) potatoes, diced

1 leek or 4 spring onions or 1 medium onion, chopped

2 tablespoons butter

1 tablespoon plain flour

1½ –2 litres (2½ – 3½ pt) stock

salt, black pepper

2 large egg yolks

4 tablespoons whipping or double cream

Cook the vegetables in the butter in a covered pan over a low heat for ten minutes, shake the pan occasionally, or stir the vegetables about, they must not brown. Add the flour, stir again, then moisten gradually, with enough stock to cover the vegetables easily. Season and simmer until the vegetables are tender, from 20-30 minutes.

Blend or sieve the soup through the *mouli-legumes,* adding enough of the remaining stock to make an agreeable consistency. Return the soup to the pan and reheat gently. Mix the yolks and cream, add a ladleful of hot soup, stirring well, then return to the pan and heat thoroughly for a few moments without boiling. Keep stirring. Taste again for seasoning. Serve with bread croutons.

Imperatives (commands), like 'cook', 'shake' 'blend', 'add'.

Certainty in the tone – very few 'you mights' or 'perhaps'. The only modal is 'must' in 'they must not brown', which is very definite.

Technical language – French word not in common use, even in recipes. Teaching the reader?

Chronological sequence – doing everything in a set order over time.

Important that everything is simple and clear. Lists of instructions as well as some short simple sentences. More compound sentences and lists than complex sentences.

Specialist words for cooking, like 'season', 'simmer', 'blend' 'stock', 'consistency'. Some French words, taken from French cuisine e.g. 'croutons' Mixture of simple words, monosyllables e.g. 'hot soup', 'low heat', 'Serve with bread' and more technical language.

# LANGUAGE THROUGH TIME

## Comparing texts – Bread and Butter Pudding from 1604 to 2004

The texts on pages 162-167 are all recipes for Bread and Butter Pudding. You have already read extracts from some of these recipes at the beginning of this unit.

Your teacher will allocate *two* texts to each pair or small group, each from different periods.

■ Read your pair of texts. Think about what's different about them and annotate them to show your ideas.

Here's a list of things you might like to think about:

- Who is likely to read this?
- How formal/informal is the writing style?
- Does it follow the format you expect from a recipe or do something different? If so, how is it different? Why do you think this might be?
- What kinds of ingredients are used and what does that tell you about the kind of world in which the recipe was written?
- What attitude is taken to the ingredients and what does this tell you?
- What kinds of words are used in the recipe?
- What is the main purpose of the recipe: to tell you how to make the dish; to make you enjoy thinking about the food; to tell you about the chef and his or her life; to tell a story?

■ Feed back your ideas to another group, or to the whole class.

## Why Have Recipe Books Changed?

On page 161 is a list of possible reasons why the language and format of recipe books may have changed so much.

■ Talk about each one in turn, deciding whether you agree or disagree and why. If you can think of other reasons, add some statements of your own. Then choose the ones that you think are most important and put them in rank order.

■ Compare your choices with those of other groups.

## Trying Out the Recipes

At the end of this unit, you might like to try making some of the puddings, following the instructions in each of the recipes. You could do it as a 'tasting' session, where you vote on the best recipe!

## COOKING THE BOOKS

### Why Have Recipe Books Changed?

| | Statement | My Rank Order |
|---|---|---|
| 1. | TV programmes on food have become really popular and have changed who is interested in food and might buy a recipe book. | |
| 2. | Nowadays people are less interested in the recipe and more interested in the 'chat' around it. | |
| 3. | People don't buy recipe books to cook food. They buy them because they want the lifestyle shown in the book. | |
| 4. | Language in books in general has become much less formal. | |
| 5. | Specialist words for cooking have changed and that's what has changed cookery books. | |
| 6. | Most people have a lot more equipment in their kitchens these days, so that's changed the recipes. | |
| 7. | Recipe books are more about advertising 'celebrity chefs' than offering the reader dishes to actually cook. | |
| 8. | Recipes used to be for 'housewives' (and servants!) – now they're for everyone, whether male or female, posh or ordinary and that's changed the way recipe books are written | |
| 9. | Foreign travel, supermarkets and more money mean that nowadays ordinary people want to try cooking a bigger range of things. | |
| 10. | Nowadays cookery books are for reading, not for teaching you how to cook | |

© English and Media Centre, 2008

LANGUAGE THROUGH TIME

## The Recipe Texts

### 1. The Lord of Devonshire His Pudding (1604)

Take manchet and slice it thin, then take dates the stones cut out, & cut in pieces, & reasins of the Sun the stones puld out, & a few currance, & marrow cut in pieces, then lay your sippets of bread in the bottome of your dish, then lay a laying of your fruit & mary on the top, then another laying of sippets of bread, so doo till your dish be full, then take creame & three eggs yolks & whites, & some Cynamon & nutmeg grated, & some sugar, beat it all well together, & pour in so much of it into the dish as it will drinke up, then set it into the oven & bake it.

*From Elinor Fettiplace's Receipt Book*

### 2. The Compleat Cook (1658)

**To make a Devonshire White-pot**

Take a pint of Cream and straine four Eggs into it, and put a little Salt and a little sliced Nutmeg, and season it with Sugar somewhat sweet; then take almost a penny Loaf of fine bread sliced very thin, and put it into a Dish that will hold it, the Cream and the Eggs being put to it; then take a handfull of Raisins of the Sun being boyled, and a little sweet Butter, so bake it.

*W. M. Anonymous, Printed by E.B. for Nath. Brook, at the Angel in Cornhill*

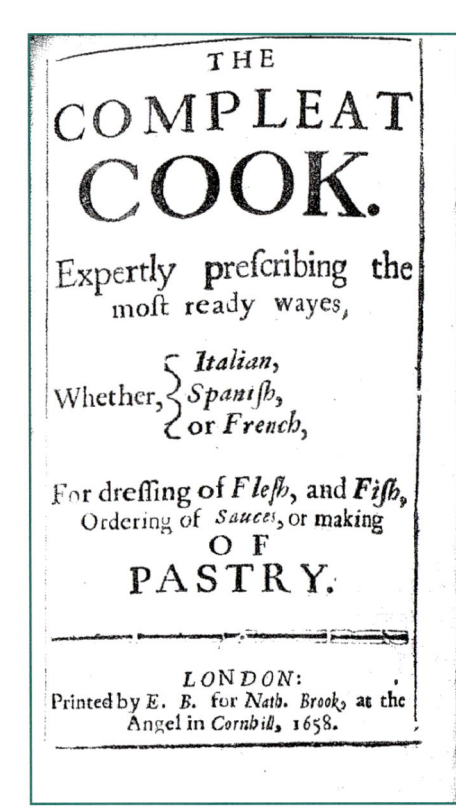

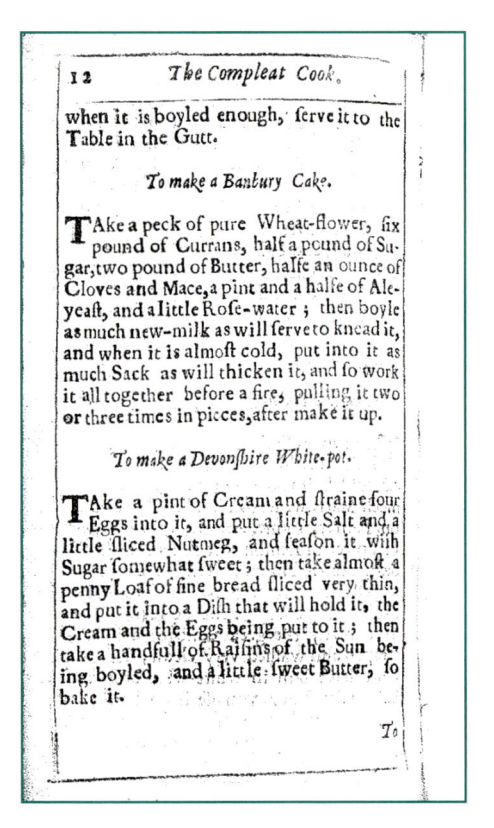

COOKING THE BOOKS

### 3. Mrs Beeton (1869)

**BAKED BREAD-AND-BUTTER PUDDING**

1255. INGREDIENTS – 9 thin slices of bread and butter, 1–1½ pint of milk, 4 eggs, sugar to taste, ¼lb. of currants, flavouring of vanilla, grated lemon-peel or nutmeg.

Mode.—Cut 9 slices of bread and butter not very thick, and put them into a pie-dish, with currants between each layer and on the top. Sweeten and flavour the milk, either by infusing a little lemon-peel in it, or by adding a few drops of essence of vanilla; well whisk the eggs, and stir these to the milk. Strain this over the bread and butter, and bake in a moderate oven for 1 hour, or rather longer. This pudding may be very much enriched by adding cream, candied peel, or more eggs than stated above. It should not be turned out, but sent to table in the pie-dish, and is better for being made about 2 hours before it is baked.

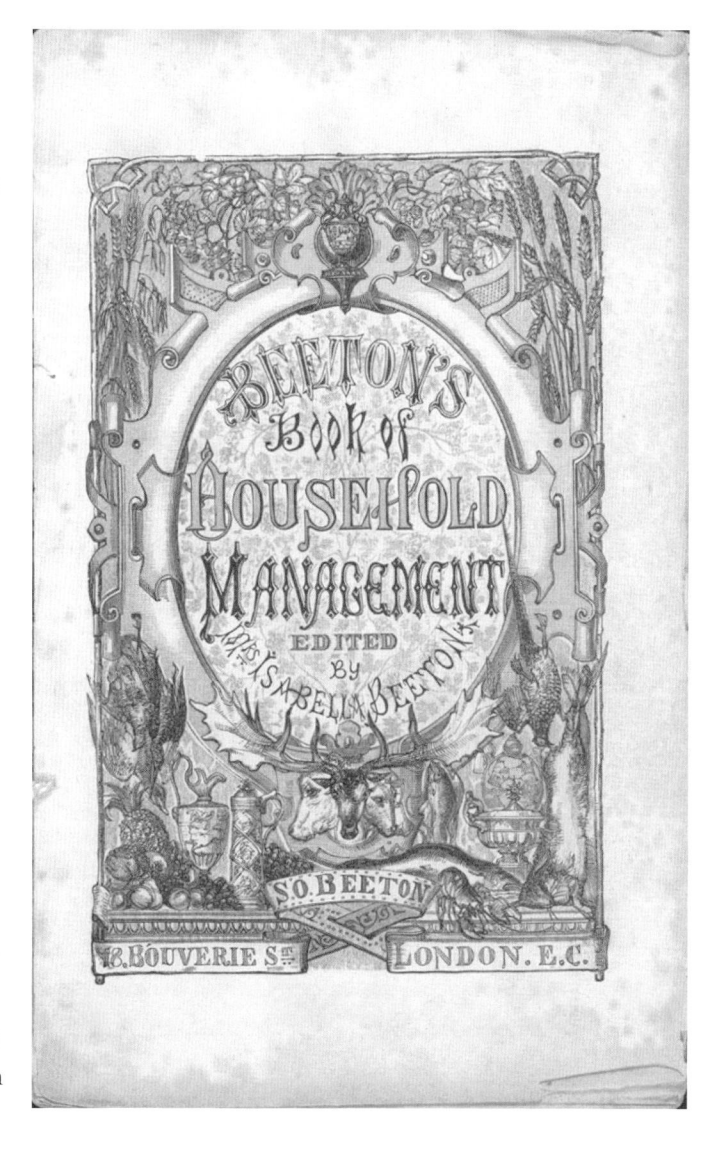

Time.—1 hour, or rather longer. Average cost, 9d.

Sufficient for 6 or 7 persons.

Seasonable at any time.

BUTTER.—Butter is indispensable in almost all culinary preparations. Good fresh butter, used in moderation, is easily digested; it is softening, nutritious, and fattening, and is far more easily digested than any other of the oleaginous substances sometimes used in its place.

### 4. Marguerite Patten (1940s)

**Bread Pudding (from 2nd World War Recipes – not quite Bread and Butter Pudding!)**

A Bread Pudding is an excellent way to use up bread. The recipe below can be varied in many ways, for example if you are short of dried fruit use a diced cooking apple or a little more marmalade. Slices of Bread Pudding are ideal to tuck into a packed meal box for a factory worker.

Cooking time: 1½ or 2 hours.

Quantity: 4 helpings

8 oz stale bread

2 oz dried fruit

2 oz grated suet or melted cooking fat

1 reconstituted dried egg

1 oz sugar

milk to mix

1 tablespoon marmalade

ground cinnamon or grated nutmeg to taste

METHOD: Put the bread into a basin, add cold water and leave for 15 minutes then squeeze dry with your fingers. Return the bread to the basin, add all the other ingredients, with enough milk to make a sticky consistency. If the spice is added last you can make quite certain you have the right amount. Put into a greased Yorkshire pudding tin and bake in the centre of a slow oven for 1½ hours or steam in a greased basin for 2 hours.

# Cooking the Books

### 5. Nigella Lawson – Nigella Bites (2001)

MY GRANDMOTHER'S GINGER-JAM BREAD & BUTTER PUDDING

Nigella: 'This recipe comes from my maternal grandmother's recipe folder, a wonderfully retro piece of design, circa late sixties, early seventies. Bread and butter pudding has, I know, gone from stodgy disparagement to fashionable rehabilitation and back to not-that-again clichédom, but I am not prepared to let any of that bother me.

This version uses brown bread rather than white, and between the buttery sandwiches is heaped chunky-hot ginger jam, sometimes sold as ginger marmalade, but most usually, if quaintly, as ginger conserve; on top is sprinkled demerara sugar mixed with aromatically warm ground ginger, the spice of the old fashioned English kitchen.

My grandmother, more austerely, used milk; I go for mostly cream: nothing creates so well that tender-bellied swell of softly set custard'.

Ingredients:

* 75g unsalted butter
* 75g sultanas
* 3 tbspns dark rum
* 10 slices brown bread
* approx. 10 x 15ml tbsps ginger conserve or marmalade
* 4 egg yolks
* 1 egg
* 3 tbspns caster sugar
* 500ml double cream
* 200ml full fat milk
* 1 tsp ground ginger
* 2 tbspns demerara sugar

Instructions:

Preheat the oven to 180C/gas mark 4.

Grease a pudding dish with a capacity of about 1.5 litres with some of the butter.

Put the sultanas in a small bowl, pour the rum over, and microwave them for 1 minute, then leave to stand. This is a good way to soak them quickly but juicily.

Make sandwiches with the brown bread, butter and ginger jam (2 tablespoons in each sandwich); you should have some butter left over to smear on the top later. Now cut the sandwiches into half triangles and arrange them evenly along the middle of the pudding dish. I put one in the dish with the point of the sandwich upwards, then one with the flat side uppermost, then with point-side uppermost and so on, then squeeze a sandwich-triangle down each side – but you do as you please. Sprinkle over the sultanas and unabsorbed rum that remains in the bowl.

Whisk the egg yolks and egg together with the caster sugar, and pour in the cream and milk. Pour this over the triangles of bread and leave them to soak up the liquid for about 10 minutes, by which time the pudding is ready to go into the oven. Smear the bread crusts that are poking out of the custard with the soft butter, mix the ground ginger and demerara sugar together and sprinkle this mixture on your buttered smeared crusts and then lightly over the rest of the pudding.

Sit the pudding dish on a baking sheet and put in the oven to cook for about 45 minutes or until the custard has set and puffed up slightly. Remove, let sit for about 10 minutes – by which time the puffiness will have deflated somewhat – and spoon out into bowls, putting a jug of custard, should you so wish, on the table to be served alongside.

### 6. Jamie Oliver – Happy Days with the Naked Chef (2004)

**Baileys and Banana Bread and Butter Pudding**

Having grown up in a pub, two of the alcoholic drinks I tried and got a taste for at a very early age were Baileys and a cocktail called a Snowball. Now I'm older I detest the taste of both of them!

Jools has a little drop of Baileys every now and again, so there's usually a bottle hanging about, and one day I had some bananas and it was as simple as that – I tried this recipe out and it was fantastic, one of the best possible twists on a bread and butter pudding.

Serves about 6

½ a loaf of pre-sliced white bread, crusts removed

55g/2oz or ¼ pack of butter, softened

140g/5oz caster sugar

seeds from 1 vanilla pod

8 free-range eggs

500ml/18fl oz double cream

565ml/1 pint milk

4 shots of Baileys

5 bananas

## Cooking the Books

4 tablespoons flaked almonds, toasted until golden

icing sugar to dust

Preheat the oven to 180°C/350°F/gas 4.

Flatten each slice of bread down as flat as possible. Butter each piece thinly but thoroughly with the softened butter, then cut the slices of bread in half and put to one side.

In a bowl whisk together the sugar, vanilla seeds and eggs till pale and fluffy, then add the cream, the milk and the Baileys and whisk until smooth. Slice up your peeled bananas and lightly toast your almonds in the preheated oven. Take an appropriately sized baking dish (or you could do individual ones) and rub the sides with a little butter. Dip each piece of bread in the egg mixture then begin to layer the bread, the sliced banana and the almonds in the baking dish. Repeat until everything has been used up, ending with a top layer of bread. Pour over the rest of your egg mixture, using your fingers to pat down the bread to make sure it soaks up all the lovely flavours.

Generously dust the top of the pudding with icing sugar and bake in the oven for around 35 minutes or until the custard has set around the outside but is just slightly wobbly in the centre. Allow it to cool and firm up slightly. Some people like to serve it with ice cream or double cream, but if you get it gooey enough in the middle then it is nice just on its own. Feel free to take this recipe in any direction you like – using raisins or dried apricots or different types of bread like brioche or pannetone.

# Cooks on TV

Comparing food programmes on TV over a period of time can tell you a lot about:

- how the world has changed
- how language has changed
- how these two things are connected.

On the DVD are three short clips from three TV celebrity chefs: Fanny Craddock, Jamie Oliver and Nigella Lawson.

### 1. Fanny Craddock, 1996

Fanny Craddock was the most famous TV cook of the 1950s and 1960s. She appeared, usually with her husband Johnnie and sometimes with an assistant. In this clip, the assistant is a young man called Simon. Fanny Craddock was known for her French-style 'gourmet' food and was educating an English audience in this glamorous, fine cooking.

### 2. Jamie Oliver, 1999

Jamie Oliver was an ordinary lad, who trained in top quality restaurants and broke into TV cooking with 'The Naked Chef'. This programme broke with traditions of food programmes. Jamie Oliver is known for wanting to make cooking democratic, so that everyone can do it, and more recently has gained huge publicity for his campaign for healthy and imaginative school meals.

### 3. Nigella Lawson, 2002

Nigella Lawson is well known for her phrase the 'domestic goddess' and for her sultry good looks and sexy approach to presenting food and cooking. She has said of herself, 'I am not a chef. I am not even a trained or professional cook. My qualification is as an eater. I cook what I want to eat – within limits...I wanted food that can be made and eaten in real life, not in perfect, isolated laboratory conditions.'

## Cooking the Books

- Brainstorm everything you notice about the clips and how they differ. You could divide it up into different aspects, with pairs looking at different things, using the chart on page 170 to record what you notice, for example:

The cook:
- age, gender and social class
- body language
- the relationship to the camera (speaking direct to camera? ignoring the camera? the camera following the presenter around?)
- how the cook addresses the viewer for example, like a teacher giving instructions, chatty, as though the audience is a friend.

The language:
- how formal or informal the language is
- how specialist or non-specialist the language is
- what kind of words are used

The programme:
- the main purpose of the programme (to educate or entertain?)
- who the programme seems to be aimed at (age? gender? social class?)
- setting (the TV studio set or location filming)
- the context in which the recipe is presented (for example just the recipe, other things going on around it)
- the ingredients and equipment
- the speed of the action and how it is edited (lots of cutting, or very little).

### What's Changed?

- Pull together all your ideas as a list of the most important things that you think have changed in the way that food programmes present recipes on TV.

- Here's one example to start you off:

    1. The language is much more chatty and everyday now – the cook speaks to the viewer as if talking to a friend.

# LANGUAGE THROUGH TIME

## Cooks on TV

| | | Fanny Craddock | Nigella Lawson | Jamie Oliver |
|---|---|---|---|---|
| **The Cook** | Age, gender, social class | | | |
| | Body language | | | |
| | Relationship to camera | | | |
| | Address to viewer | | | |
| **The Language** | Formal or informal? | | | |
| | Specialist or non-specialist? | | | |
| | Kinds of words | | | |
| **The Programme** | Purpose & audience | | | |
| | Setting | | | |
| | Context | | | |
| | Ingredients & equipment | | | |
| | Speed of action & editing | | | |

# COOKING THE BOOKS

## Suggestions for Your Own Writing

1. Write your own recipe for another dish, in the style of one of the cookery writers you have looked at: Nigella Lawson, Jamie Oliver, Marguerite Patten or Mrs Beeton. You could take something simple like scrambled eggs on toast, or a chocolate milkshake, or a fruit smoothie.

■ Before you start, look back at the recipe you are imitating and make a list of features, that is everything you notice about the content and the style. Here are a few ideas to start you off:

**Nigella**
- Tells a story about where she got the recipe from before she starts
- Gives a strong opinion of her own about food

**Jamie**
- Gives some personal details from his family life

**Marguerite Patten**
- No use of first person. No sense of a personal voice (we don't get any sense of what the writer is like from the way the recipe is written)
- Focuses on how to make ingredients go a long way

**Mrs Beeton**
- Starts straight in with list of ingredients

■ When you start writing your recipe, use your list of features to help remind you what you're trying to imitate.

2. Write the story of your Shakespeare play for SATs, or another book you've been reading in class in the style of a recipe. Choose whether you want to do it as a simple recipe or adopt the style of one of the cookery writers you've looked at.

3. Write your own comic sketch, parodying (or making fun of) one of the TV chefs shown in the video clips and perform it for your class, or video it. Comic parodies often:

- exaggerate
- make things absurd
- put together things that seem ridiculous, for example whisk your family's socks together into a light, fragrant soufflé
- make up words or use words incorrectly, for example sprangle the mixture with plaster sugar
- use comic let-downs (bathos), for example stir, whisk, and flavour this delectable mixture of deliciously smooth earwax.

# Extension Activities

## What's a Pudding?

Here's a modern dictionary definition of the word 'pudding':

> Pudding [pooding] n boiled or baked mixture of flour, suet etc; boiled sweetened rice or sago; any solid sweet dish; a batter; a type of sausage;

- When it was first used in English, the word 'pudding' only meant savoury sausage. Nowadays we mostly use it for sweet desserts, although it still survives in its savoury version in 'black pudding', 'yorkshire pudding' and 'steak and kidney pudding'.

- Look at the text at the bottom of the page. It is an entry from an etymological dictionary, a dictionary that lists all the different ways in which a word has been used over time. It tries to explain how words came into use in English. There are two possible theories about how 'pudding' came into the English Language. Try to work each out. Use this key to help you:

    c. = approximately
    W.Gmc = West Germanic
    cf = see the entry on this other word for more information
    O.E. = Old English
    V.L. = Vulgar Latin, the everyday speech of ordinary Romans, rather than written Latin
    L. = Latin
    O.Fr = Old French
    Fr. = French
    Ger. = German
    Low Ger.
    dial. = dialect
    Eng. = English
    Ir. = Irish

- Which theory do you prefer? Present your favourite theory to another group, giving reasons for your choice.

> c.1305, "a kind of sausage: the stomach or one of the entrails of a pig, sheep, etc., stuffed with minced meat, suet, seasoning, boiled and kept till needed," perhaps from a W.Gmc. stem *pud- "to swell" (cf. O.E. *puduc* "a wen," Westphalian dial. *puddek* "lump, pudding," Low Ger. *pudde-wurst* "black pudding," Eng. dial. pod "belly," also cf. *pudgy*). Other possibility is that it is from O.Fr. *boudin* "sausage," from V.L. **botellinus*, from L. *botellus* "sausage" (change of Fr. b- to Eng. p- presents difficulties, but cf. *purse*). The modern sense had emerged by 1670, from extension to other foods boiled or steamed in a bag or sack. Ger. *pudding*, Fr. *pouding*, Swed. *pudding*, Ir. *putog* are from Eng. *Puddinghead* "amiable stupid person" is attested from 1851.
>
> *www.etymonline.com/index.php?l=p&p=36*

## COOKING THE BOOKS

### A Parody of Food Programmes: Posh Nosh – Bread AND Butter Pudding

*Posh Nosh*, starring Richard E Grant and Arabella Weir was an award-winning comedy series shown on BBC2 in 2002. The 10-minute programmes parodied (or made fun of) the many cookery programmes and television chefs on air at the time.

■ Read the item below from the *Posh Nosh* pages on the BBC website on 'Bread AND butter pudding.' You can view the video online at http://www.bbc.co.uk/comedy/poshnosh/recipes/breadbutter_video.shtml

■ Talk about what it is getting you to laugh at.

■ Pick out your three favourite examples and, in each case, explain to the class what it was parodying and what you found funny about it.

■ After discussing the extract, write your own parody of a food programme of your choice, in which you exaggerate the particular features of the programme and the style of the presenter's language, for example Jamie Oliver's mockney language, Nigella's sumptuous and luxuriant use of language or Hugh Fearnley-Whittingstall's jolly enthusiasm for everything home-produced.

**Extract from Posh Nosh**

**Simon**     What's the secret of a great bread and butter pudding? The bread? The butter? The pudding?

No. It's all in the 'and'. That's why we call this dish Bread AND Butter Pudding.

We created it in the late twentieth century for the opening of our restaurant, The Quill and Tassel at Bray. Was it Nigel Havers who christened it 'the dessert of the nineties'? Possibly. So many people claim that honour, we can't tell the myth from the truth. Perhaps it was Stephen Fry, who dined with us first in 1997 and will return when his filming commitments allow. 'The dessert of the nineties' – it certainly has the style and wit we associate with my man Steve!

Our inspiration came from the first recorded recipe for 'bred puddyng', included in Eliza Brampton's 'Boke Of Cokery' published in 1571. We bought it at a Sotheby's auction for £17,500, to save it for the nation. Our house, Crowe Hall, is open to the public during the second week of August every year. Come and visit our safe and admire it. No beards or children, naturally.

'Take bred. Frye hit yn oyle. Grynde hit with reysons and drawe hit. Claryfy honye with gleyr of eyron and water. Scom hit clenel and put hit to that othir.' We could go on. And we will. 'Do therto clovy, macez and gynger mynsed. Loke hit be stondyng and floresch hit with annes in confite.'

That's what we did. But what do you do if you're ordinary? The first thing you do is buy yourself a bottle of 1986 Barsac. The chalky soil at Barsac produces the world's finest sweet wines. Go there and rub a hundred grams between your thumb and fingertips. Sniff it. It's the source of vinicultural greatness. Sniff it again. Sniff it hard. Lick it. Go on. Now swallow. Swallow that soil and you'll understand why we made it compulsory. You can't order our Bread AND Butter Pudding without an '86 Barsac.

Some rules are made to be broken. That is not one of them.

## Cooking the Books

Ingredients:
29 currants from Corinth
Cognac
10 soupçons of milk, organic cow's, wholly pasteurised, utterly non-homogenised and totally semi-skimmed
1 pinche of Caster sugar
1 demerara sugar
Vanilla essence
3 layers of trusted organic wholemeal bread, thinly abused
2 of Arthur Legg-Bourke's eggs
Fennel, close-shaved

The most important ingredient in our 'AND' is the currants. For two thousand years, Greek men with moussaka-flavoured moustaches have dried grapes on sheets in the sun south of Corinth. Only buy Greek currants, from Greek men, in Greece. We do our Currant Run in early May, when the mimosa is just out, the hotels are half-empty and the boys are just starting to put their shorts back on...

**Minty**  Splash-drop three high-tablespoons of cognac into a handmade mixing-bowl. Applique the currants. Leave them in there for three to six months to make sure they're completely exasperated. Meanwhile, slice your loaf thinly and let the slices breathe. We put them in a basket by the tennis court.

For the custard, hob-heat your milk soupçons till they enquire. Wood-blend fifty grams of organic caster sugar. We wood-blend to Purcell. Though long-dead, his music soothes and thrills in just the right proportions.

Leak approximately 2.5 millilitres of Madagascan vanilla essence. It's easily available in all good foodshops in Madagascar. Pour in the beaten eggs and fluff diplomatically till the custard's thoroughly relaxed.

Butter an early Conran ovenproof dish, waltzing it round like so. Now take an ounce of brown sugar (28 eurogrammes).

**Quentin**  Absolve your bread slices in layers, perplexing each layer with currants and demerara sugar, taking care to ravel in the usual way. Aga-bake for 58 minutes at torchmark 5.

De-Aga.

**Simon**  What you see now is what we served on the opening night of the Quill and Tassel. Yes, it was sensational. But something was missing. You have to be utterly honest at a time like that. Honest with yourself, your staff and your audience. And, above all, honest with your food. I couldn't look at those marvellous currants. I knew I'd let them down.

At four the next morning, I sat upright in bed. I rushed into Minty's room.

**LANGUAGE THROUGH TIME**

**Minty**  We sleep in separate rooms on account of the snoring!

**Simon**  I woke her up and said one word. 'Fennel.'

At lunchtime, I scattered a palmful of closely-shaved fennel on our Bread AND Butter Pudding.

That was it.

Now we had the Bread AND Butter Pudding so admired by Steve Fry.

And, dare I say it, Nig Havers.